The Politics of Local Government

The Politics of Local Government

Governing in Small Towns and Suburbia

Barry E. Truchil

LEXINGTON BOOKS
Lanham • Boulder • New York • London

Published by Lexington Books
An imprint of The Rowman & Littlefield Publishing Group, Inc.
4501 Forbes Boulevard, Suite 200, Lanham, Maryland 20706
www.rowman.com

Unit A, Whitacre Mews, 26-34 Stannary Street, London SE11 4AB

British Library Cataloguing in Publication Information Available

Library of Congress Cataloging-in-Publication Data

Names: Truchil, Barry E., author.
Title: The politics of local government : governing in small towns and suburbia / Barry E. Truchil.
Description: Lanham, Maryland : Lexington Books, [2017] | Includes bibliographical references and index.
Identifiers: LCCN 2017044238 (print) | LCCN 2017052083 (ebook) | ISBN 9781498520454 (Electronic) | ISBN 9781498520447 (cloth : alk. paper)
Subjects: LCSH: Local government—United States. | Local budgets—United States. | Politics, Practical—United States. | Political corruption—United States.
Classification: LCC JS331 (ebook) | LCC JS331 .T78 2017 (print) | DDC 320.80973—dc23
LC record available at https://lccn.loc.gov/2017044238

♾™ The paper used in this publication meets the minimum requirements of American National Standard for Information Sciences—Permanence of Paper for Printed Library Materials, ANSI/NISO Z39.48-1992.

Printed in the United States of America

To Bernadette, Rachael, and Aaron

Contents

Acknowledgments

Much of the research in the book was made possible due to Paid Research Leaves and Summer Fellowships from Rider University, where I am a faculty member in the Department of Sociology. I am also appreciative of the comments from discussants and others during professional conferences in sociology and political science, where aspects of the manuscript were given as papers. Thanks also to the anonymous reviewer for this publisher, who provided good ideas on how to improve the manuscript. Robert Wharton, who served with me as a fellow member of Council, was kind enough to review my case studies for accuracy. Finally, deep appreciation has to be expressed to Bernadette West, my wife and partner through all these years, as she carefully read each chapter more than once and provided meaningful comments and editing throughout this process. It is to Bernadette and our children, Rachael and Aaron, that I dedicate this book.

Introduction

This book is about the workings and politics of local government in suburban and small-town settings. It addresses key issues and problems that elected officials in local government face as well as the political processes and conflicts that can take place along the way. In addition to incorporating scholarly research in sociology, political science and other disciplines, the book has an added dimension; having served as an elected official in a small town for fourteen years, I draw upon my years of holding elected office in discussing issues using specific "case studies" in each of the chapters. The specific examples from my elected office experiences are presented in *italics* throughout the book. These instances are thus my own experiences used as examples to illustrate some of the more general issues discussed in each chapter.

I was an elected member of council in a small town from 1992 to 2006, and served as council president from 1994 to 2004. I never intended to run for office. In fact, I really did not know much about my local government when I moved to the area. However, less than two years after having moved into town, I received a letter in the mail stating that the owner of the property next door to my home wanted to have her house rezoned as a commercial property in order to house her psychotherapy practice there. The letter noted that there would be a hearing by the Zoning Hearing Board to consider this request. A meeting with my neighbors revealed that everyone opposed this potential change. Concerns centered on a likely increase in traffic and the worry that a new business might threaten the residential character of the street. We decided to go en masse *to the meeting to voice our objections. In the process, I became the unofficial leader of this effort. We succeeded in stopping the rezoning effort and afterwards, I was also told about a vacancy on the Zoning Hearing Board.*

I considered the opportunity and decided to apply for the position. When I applied, I was told by a "community leader" *that my application would go more smoothly if I changed my party affiliation from Democrat to Republican. There was a heavy Republican presence in the town's government and on the various boards; in fact, at that time, there had been only two Democrats in the history of the town to serve on the Borough Council. I indicated I was staying Democratic, but since no one else applied, I eventually was appointed to the Zoning Hearing Board. Two years later, I ran for office as a Democrat and won my first election by 12 votes! At the time I ran for office, there were competing factions within the Republican Party, and with the support of some traditionally Republican groups (as well as Democrats), I was able to win.*

In our town, a large number of residents belonging to the Republican and Democratic parties were deeply interested in preserving open space, maintaining—through legislation—the historic character of the town's historic district, and introducing measures that help protect the environment. Others, who were not part of this coalition of Republicans and Democrats simply did not want to see their taxes increased, and some may have preferred to see more development in town. The former faction, of which I was a part, prevailed.

In another two years, I was chosen by my fellow members of council to become council president, perhaps because I was very open to supporting the goals of preserving open space and maintaining the historic character of the town. For a brief time, the council was made up of a majority of Democrats, but the same competing coalitions continued to remain. I continued to serve until 2004.

My elected experience provided me with the opportunity to learn about various aspects of the governing process at the local governmental level in a small town, including the need for careful budgeting, and the importance of providing residents with a safe town. Perhaps most important, was the importance of balancing competing interests—those who wanted to encourage more growth and development in town (a view typically held by organized business in town), and those who wanted to maintain the existing residential character of the town. These forces played out within a larger political context where people generally wanted to avoid tax increases, making fiscal prudence the *modus operandi* of governing in this small town.

As a sociology professor, I found myself often drawing upon my government experiences in classes. Eventually, as I sought to incorporate readings in my courses on the politics of local government in small suburban towns, I was struck by the lack of work in this area. This book is an attempt to fill that void by integrating my experiences governing in my small town within the context of existing interdisciplinary literature on the subject of local government. While I incorporate experiences in my town as "case studies" designed to illustrate various aspects of local government in one small town, I believe many aspects are applicable to other local governmental settings in small towns and suburbia. Indeed, these case studies are examples of many of the issues raised in the scholarly literature.

There are a number of studies that have focused on small towns, urban and suburban neighborhoods that are considered classics in the sociological literature. Almost all of them were written before 1960, and these studies discuss local government in general terms. For example, in Robert Lynd and Helen Merrell Lynd's *Middletown*, they examined a small city in the early twentieth century. They discussed many aspects of community structure and culture, but offered scant treatment of local government. They noted the cynicism of local residents toward their local government and saw local leaders as corrupt (1956: 425). However, the inner workings of government, such as the strategies employed, the "tricks of the trade," and budgeting and legal procedures, among others, were not addressed.

In *Small Town in Mass Society* by Arthur Vidich and Joseph Bensman, the authors examined a small town during the 1950s. They captured the local discussions of residents on political issues as well as the gossip and conspiracy theories that obsess residents and political leaders (1968: 109). They observed that political discussions tended to focus on the personalities of those in office and that it was the goal of everyone it seemed to keep taxes and spending low (p. 110). Because their concerns primarily focused on the structural and cultural aspects of the town, the workings of local government were not part of their study.

In *Small Town and the Nation* by Don Martindale and R. Gaelen Hanson, the authors examined a small town in Minnesota during the 1960s. They portray a town that is self-contained, but also interconnected to the larger region; however, there is little discussion of local government.

Herbert Gans conducted two landmark studies on towns and neighborhoods. In *the Levittowners*, he provides a profile of the people of Levittown, looks at the development of this suburban area, how people lived and their relationship to the larger city. Gans indeed discusses politics and dedicates a large part of the book to it. Because Levittown was a nascent community, he focused on the rise of political parties in the area, the growth of municipal services and the debates that occurred among residents regarding the kind of local government that should be established. His treatment of the intersection of the development of a political culture and the rise of a local government, however, does not provide an insider's view of that local government. In *Urban Villagers*, he examines one neighborhood community in Boston and treats it as if it was a small town. Here again, he discusses politics, especially how working-class and middle-class residents define the role of government differently (1982: 163–176). The way government works, again, is not part of the discussion.

These and other community-based studies offer meaningful contributions to the study of structure and culture in small towns and suburban areas at a time when there was a demographic shift from the city to the suburbs. It is understandable that the questions posed by these authors had more to do with the development of new regions. The issues faced by local government officials were not a primary concern.

The growth of suburban areas has continued to inspire research on suburbia as a region. In *Crabgrass Frontier: The Suburbanization of the United States*, Kenneth Jackson examines the rise of the suburban regions of the country. He examines their development and how economic and political forces shaped this development.

In his book, *The Suburbs*, John Palen reviews many forms of local governments (83,186) throughout the United States, including county, municipal, townships, villages and school districts, among others (1995: 176). And while there appears to be a surfeit of formats for local government, Palen notes that the current system with such diversity appears to work. However, the exact nature of how these local governments work is not considered.

In *The American Suburb,* Jon C. Teaford describes the fragmentation of local government as the essence of suburbia and small towns (2008: 123). In an earlier book, he also discussed how local suburban neighborhoods work to separate themselves from urban governments in order to establish their own exclusivity and services (1979: 76–104). While he sees local government as a form of "power to the people," the inner workings of local government are once again not part of the discussion.

Robert Beauregard's *When America Became Suburban* examines the growth of America's suburbs between 1945 and 1970 as part of America's Short Century, where the United States became a global power and witnessed a period of prosperity and mass consumerism (2006: 1–19). While local governments in the suburbs are seen as a necessary part of growth and development of suburban areas, the conflicts and nuances of how local government addressed development are not part of his larger thesis.

A smaller body of literature does specifically address the work of local government. Duany, Plater-Zyberg and Speck in *Suburban Nation: The Rise of Sprawl and the Decline of the American Dream* look at local government and its role in writing or rewriting regulations to control suburban sprawl (2000: 237–269). Similar themes of local government taking on developers and suburban sprawl are also discussed by Logan and Molotch (1987), Siskind (2006) and Gendron and Domhoff (2009), among others. Their contributions are noted in the current research, as well as other specific writings on budgeting, zoning and various initiatives that local government officials undertake.

There are works within the field of political science that examine types of government. Of course, Alexis de Toqueville's *Democracy in America* would be an obvious starting point. Toqueville distinguished the township, or local government, from the national level (2000: 56–73). He recognized more local levels of government as central to democracy in the United States. Robert Dahl's classic work on New Haven, Connecticut similarly builds on the tradition of examining local government as a lynchpin of democracy (Dahl, 1961).

There is a body of literature on local government focusing on the county level (Sly, 1967; Marando and Thomas, 1977; Duncombe, 1966; Bollens, *et al.*, 1960). While the services that county governments provide are broader than those provided by small-town governments, this literature offers some insights that are discussed in this book. For the most part, however, this research tends to have been written prior to 1970 when most suburban areas were in a growth mode. Since the 1980s, many local governments have been working to slow growth as a means to control unfettered suburban sprawl. Where appropriate, the current research draws upon some of the ways that local governments act to control growth.

While a review of more recent books on state and local government reveals some discussion of different aspects of local government, only a few focus on the aspects of the inner workings of local government (Dye, 2008; Smith, *et al.,* 2005; Lorch, 2000). Therefore, while some treatment of local government is given in the literature, the current research contributes to the field by providing an insider's discussion of substantive issues confronting local government from the perspective of those actually involved in the process of governing.

The current research presented here is also unique in that it is firmly placed within the context of "public sociology" advanced by Michael Burawoy. He proffered the idea of public sociology at his Presidential Address at the Annual Sociological Association meetings, when he served as president of the American Sociological Association in 2004 (Burawoy, 2005). Public sociology is contrasted with "professional sociology"; the latter is a form of academic sociology that addresses the theoretical and methodological concerns raised by other professional sociologists. It is primarily intended for academic sociologists. Public sociology, on the other hand, is a relatively recent form of intellectual inquiry. It focuses on the day-to-day issues that members of society face and uses active sociological inquiry to help answer questions and solve issues. It seeks to contribute to the sociological literature while making the research accessible to larger audiences at the same time.

> Public sociology engages diverse publics, reaching beyond the university to enter into an ongoing dialogue with these publics about fundamental values.

> This public sociology is distinguished by its use of reflexive knowledge and its appeal beyond the university. (Land, 2008: 509)

The goals of public sociology have sparked ongoing interest and debate (Clawson, *et al.*, 2007; Agger, 2007). It is clearly a trend that is influencing new research. The current research is part of this new tradition as it draws upon the routines of local government. And while the research will be of use to social scientists, the goal is also to make the work accessible to the larger public. Having held elected office for more than a dozen years, my personal/professional boundaries have become more and more porous. This combination of civic engagement with research is thus within the spirit of public sociology.

Case studies drawn from my experiences as an elected official are woven throughout the current research. I have actively participated in all aspects of the governing process. I have had access to all financial, legal and other forms of data used in decision-making processes. As council president, I negotiated contracts with employees, including the police department, presided over council meetings, negotiated on behalf of the town with elected officials from other municipalities, mediated conflicts between different elected and non-elected constituencies such as between business owners and residents, addressed competing demands for government resources among community entities such as between police and fire departments, and worked with lawyers on a host of government-related issues. I undertook a variety of creative initiatives at the local government level (e.g., the decision to have 100% of our municipal energy come from 100% renewable resources). These experiences serve as valuable case studies on how local government works and faces the challenges in its efforts to bring about change. By drawing on the existing literature on local government and combining it with participant observation from the vantage point of an elected local official, my unique position provides a context within which to make a significant contribution to the literature on local government as well as work within the nascent tradition of "public sociology."

Adding to the literature on local government remains an important task. There is considerable work being done on city government, and important contributions have been made from this research. In 1979, Stanfield described the conditions that gave rise to an "awakening of small town America" (1979: 36). Governments in small towns and suburbia have been seen to have a different constellation of issues facing them (Rehfuss, 1977: 111–120). Moreover, according to the *Municipal Year Book* for 2009, more than half of all municipalities have less than 10,000 residents, and over one-third of municipalities have less than 5,000 residents (ICMA, 2009: x–xi). While some may debate former house speaker Tip O'Neill's dictum, "All Politics is Local," insights into the inner workings of government in small towns and suburbia will increase our awareness of this form of governing. My unique involvement as a member of council—particularly ten years as council president—has provided me with both experiences and perspectives to increase understanding.

Chapter 1 focuses on the financial aspects of local government. The myth of a balanced budget and the tricks of fund accounting are exposed and used to demonstrate how the financial operations of local government are made to appear mystical and inaccessible to residents of the town. The conflicts created by different departments within government are discussed, for example the conflict between the police, which seeks to expand their budget under conditions focused on the need to keep costs and taxes under control and local government officials. This chapter serves as a primer for deciphering both a town's budget and strategies that can be used to discern whether or not the town needs additional money.

Chapter 2 focuses on political conflict at the local level drawing upon the concept of the "local growth machine" as developed by Logan and Molotch (Logan and Molotch, 1987: 50–98). Logan and Molotch identify two main forces at work in local politics: the local growth machine, which seeks to intensify land use through increased development in the town, and local residents and their allies, who seek to preserve the character of the town that they love. The historical genesis of the growth coalition and how it influences local government officials are addressed. The role of local government in these disputes is discussed as well as approaches that local government can use to control development. The types of political weapons at government's disposal are delineated, as well as the limitations local government faces in seeking to control growth.

Chapter 3 explores ways in which towns can implement progressive politics. The chapter focuses on progressive actions local governments can initiate to make positive differences in the lives of residents within the community, including environmental initiatives, increasing public exposure to the arts and partnering with nonprofit organizations to provide low-income housing. The rationales for those who oppose such measures are also examined.

Chapter 4 examines the concept of corruption in local government. While most attention to corruption has focused on clearly illegal activities such as bribery or personal gain from government actions, the chapter also looks at what could be seen as legal forms of corruption, or "corruption by any other name." A concluding chapter reviews the main points raised in the book.

The challenges in writing a book like this lie in linking personal experiences with the theories and concepts in the literature. In certain areas (e.g., the growth machine), there is an abundance of research, while in other areas (e.g., the financial workings of local government), the literature is sparse. In some cases, more emphasis has been placed on personal experiences, which mainly appear as "case studies" throughout the book, with the hope that these examples will be useful for subsequent work in an area that has received very little attention in recent years.

Chapter 1

The Myth of a Balanced Budget

Government at all levels—national, state or local level—must have a budget in order to plan expected revenues as well as necessary expenditures. A budget also allows governments to then compare what was planned with actual expenditures so that future budgets can use available money as efficiently as possible.

Local government budgets, especially in small towns and suburbs, are not as elaborate as federal or state budgets because the scope of operations is smaller. Local governments do not have the extensive programs that can be seen at these other levels of government, such as health departments, welfare offices, etc.; however, they still have to provide important services, including providing security to their residents, plowing the snow-covered streets, etc.

Given that the public entrusts government to manage its money wisely and effectively, it makes sense to require government to prepare and balance a budget each year. Indeed, everyone, whether as individuals or in families, needs to manage money wisely. While it makes good sense for individuals and families to keep their spending at least within the range of revenue coming in, no one comes in to check their books at the end of the year. In fact, what individuals and families do with their own money is really no one else's business. These are considered to be private matters.

Government, which is using taxpayers' money, however, is held to a higher standard, and as such, is audited annually by a firm of independent certified public accountants. After all, government should not be wasting taxpayers' money; they have the right to make sure that their money is spent wisely. Since government money is the public's money, how that money is used is, by necessity, a public issue, at least within the context of American politics and culture.

Moreover, government should be able to live within its means. Spending more money than you take in only leads to borrowing, where the interest and principal has to be paid in future years, thereby tying up future money. If a local government is living beyond its means in a given year, then it will probably do so in subsequent years. That situation would mean having to raise taxes or taking out loans to cover the extra spending, along with having to incorporate the additional interest and principal payments in subsequent budgets. On the other hand, if a government had very large surpluses each year, citizens may want a reduction in taxes. The ideal scenario is that the government taxes its citizens at just the right amount to cover its expenditures (leaving aside for the moment whether those expenditures are wise ones or in the general interest).

The federal government is not obligated to have a balanced budget, because there are extenuating circumstances such as war or job creation programs that potentially can arise due to crises of some kind. Being bound to a balanced budget can seriously undermine the ability of the federal government to address the needs of citizens or to provide for their security. The president and Congress may take advantage of this ability by approving tax cuts or authorizing expenditures for various reasons even though they know it will only exacerbate the deficit. Some political groups call for a balanced budget amendment to the Constitution, but such an amendment would have to allow the federal government to have the flexibility to react to sudden crises and needs.

State governments have to provide a balanced budget. State laws determine whether or not local governments have to have a balanced budget. In Pennsylvania, the state government has passed a set of rules for local governments (e.g., Borough Code) that includes rules regarding budgeting. Local governments, whether municipalities, townships or boroughs in the state, are not necessarily required to have a balanced budget, but it is a general practice to present one to the community when annual budgets are approved. If a municipality shows a budget that shows profit, residents will understandably raise concerns that taxes may be too high. Unless there are extenuating circumstances, there would be little sense in budgeting a deficit. While a chronic deficit may support a case for raising taxes, it would also suggest that local officials are not spending within their means.

There are numerous state laws that pertain to local governmental budgets, including the need for citizen input. For example, in Pennsylvania, Borough Code, Section 1308 specifies that a local government must advertise a proposed budget thirty days prior to its adoption for the next year in a local newspaper so that citizens can learn about it and comment on it. On a January through December budget cycle, the preliminary budget is usually presented at a fall meeting. An announcement about the pending budget must be advertised in the local newspaper and then it is formally adopted at the December meeting. This process allows residents (those few lucky ones able to find the advertisement in the obscure sections of the newspapers, where such announcements are placed) to examine the proposed budget and have input if they so choose at the meeting where the budget is discussed and approved. This budget also takes into account any new tax increase, but the tax rates are approved separately after the budget is approved. Tax rates must also be duly advertised prior to the meeting (in the same obscure sections of the paper). Many towns also post minutes of meetings and copies of proposed ordinances and budgets at their municipal buildings and on their websites as well, though most residents are unaware of this practice. Informed citizens (or even elected officials opposing majority decisions) could nonetheless mobilize other citizens by "getting the word out" on budget issues and thereby encourage their participation at subsequent government meetings.

Most budget practices are similar for local governments, large and small. O'Toole, Marshall and Grewe examined local government budget practices and found commonalities in the way budgeting takes place (1996: 25–29). Most municipalities have a budget office that plays a key role in carrying out budgeting activities. In small towns, an ad hoc group consisting of the bookkeeper, manager and elected officials who make up the Budget Committee often plays this role. Some local governments may use a two-year budget cycle, but most encompass only one year (O'Toole, Marshall and Grewe, 1996: 26). Based primarily on previous trends, the staff makes estimates on future revenues and expenses. Most towns use a line-item budget, but some towns compare each month's expenditures with a model that assumes that one-twelfth of the annual budget will be spent each month; any department, whether police or streets, can be monitored to determine if they are keeping within the budget. Expenditures such as snow removal are naturally more seasonal.

The budget process actually begins several months prior to introduction of the budget when the Budget Committee, assisted by the bookkeeper, managers and treasurer, begins its review of revenues and expenditures during the summer or fall months. This review examines whether projected revenues have been met and whether expenditures are in line with what was allocated. The bookkeeper will write a report with all the pertinent figures, comparing the current year to previous ones. Any discrepancies between projections and actual revenues and expenditures would then be examined more closely. For example, a recession might cause the mercantile tax to be lower than projected. A boom economy might have the reverse effect. An unusual amount of snow might adversely affect the budget line for snow removal. The police chief or town manager may have gone on an unanticipated spending spree. In any case, the committee has to understand deviations from the previous year's forecast and identify which deviations are controllable (e.g., choices made by employees) and which are linked to external factors beyond the control of local government (e.g., harsh winters, economic cycles and insurance costs).

These unanticipated costs demonstrate the need for local governments to have some money stashed away to cover unanticipated expenditures, just as households must have savings to cover unanticipated expenses. While a balanced budget assumes government spends what it brings in as revenues, it too needs extra revenues for those years that have additional expenses. Indeed, a vice president from Moody's Services argued that municipalities should have sufficient reserves and maintain a plan for them to sustain communities during economic downturns (Incarvaia, 2003: 8). The goal is to show a balanced budget while actually having a little surplus built into it. For example, allocating more money for snow removal can do this, or underestimating sources of revenue, such as real estate transfer taxes. Hence, a balanced budget is a desired goal; however, from a practical standpoint, it may be a strategic way to hide a surplus within the budget to cover future unanticipated expenses.

The Budget Committee then has to determine what additional money will be needed for the following year. For example, budgets may need to factor in employee raises. Usually, local governments attempt to stay within the norm for what most people in the surrounding area are getting in terms of increases in salary, as long as those raises are affordable. An initial impulse might be to try to limit increases to save money, but employees have families with bills to pay like everyone else, and how employees are paid impacts how they feel about their job, and ultimately their overall job performance.

While an examination of previous budgets can serve as a prudent guide for forecasting revenues and expenditures, there are always "guesstimates" that must be made in the process. No one has a foolproof way to predict snowfall amounts, so the cost for winter plowing is always an estimate. Likewise, it is not possible to predict the amount of property taxes that will be generated from the sales of homes, the revenue from traffic tickets, or even how many residents will/will not pay their taxes. Data from previous years can be a useful guide and help keep estimates within the ballpark. There is always some guesswork because there are conditions that are outside anyone's control. Padding a little surplus into the "balanced" budget is a very good way of protecting the town from unanticipated shortfalls of revenue or unexpected expenses.

The fiscal year of most municipalities runs January through December, even though the state government and school districts may run from July through June. The main source of revenue—property taxes—tends to start coming in by the end of March. As a consequence, government officials must make sure that they not only have enough money to make it through the fiscal year, but also to the end of March, when tax revenue starts coming in. This amount is often called "carry over." Money from the previous year's budget is carried over to pay the bills and payroll from January through March. When tax revenues come in, a year's worth is anticipated for April through December plus the next year's carry over. Everything is supposed to balance out, at least theoretically. The revenue stream therefore does not completely mesh with the fiscal year. That is not to say there is additional money coming in. Revenues from various sources, including traffic violations, mercantile (business) taxes, amusement (e.g., golf courses, amusement parks, etc.) taxes and transfer taxes from the sales of property arrive throughout the fiscal year. Revenue from traffic violations comes in monthly (though the amount varies from month to month), but revenue from other sources arrives more randomly. The timing of some revenue is linked to when the companies hired to collect it send the money, as in the specialized taxes, such as an amusement tax, that require specialists to collect them from businesses. Others, like the real estate transfer tax, depend on when houses and other properties are sold. Ordinarily, expenditures are far greater than revenues during the months of January through March, and government officials tend to see a big decline in the general fund during these leaner periods. The expectation is that new taxes will come in before the existing "carry over" is depleted. Padding a little surplus into the budget is a good way to ensure a sufficient "carry over."

In order to meet the needs of residents for security, services and cultural needs, local governments must have a stable revenue stream. To have the necessary revenues while maintaining a balanced budget, local governments have three options: raise revenues by increasing the tax rate or other optimization strategies, develop new sources of revenue, including increasing one's tax base, or reduce the existing level of services (Gianakis and McCue, 1999: 113). Government officials can also try to use their resources as efficiently as possible. One must assume a continuous drive to use government resources as efficiently as possible all the time. However, there are always new ways to use money wisely.

Most municipalities receive revenue from a host of sources, including property taxes, mercantile tax from local businesses, real estate transfer taxes, building permits, amusement taxes (from golf clubs, video games, etc.), traffic citations, parking tickets, and local service taxes (such as emergency/ambulatory services). While these sources of revenue have rates that are fixed by state government, the local municipality controls property taxes based on real estate holdings in the town and the bulk of revenue comes from this tax.

In many small towns, property taxes make up the largest source of income (Christensen and Hogen-Esch, 2006: 285). Property tax can be defined simply as a levy "at a uniform rate on the capital value of property as revealed by the current market" (Gaffney, 1971: 410). A municipality levies a millage against the assessed value of properties. This tax is the bane of most property owners, and discussion and news regarding tax increases at the local level largely pertain to the property tax. The use of property taxes for schools is another concern for residents since school districts in most suburban towns have their own taxing authority. While the property tax can generally be unpopular with homeowners, and it certainly varies from state to state, it is, in effect, a good way for a local government to raise revenues fairly. It is a progressive tax, and its proponents go back to James Madison (Gaffney, 1971: 408; see also Musgrave, 1974). As Steven Ginsberg has written, "our income tax system may be geared to collect more from the affluent, but it includes numerous loopholes that allow the rich to slip out of paying an amount truly commensurate with their wealth. The property tax picks up where the income tax leaves off" (1997: 33). In other words, the more a property is worth, the more the property owner pays in property tax. If property taxes are reduced, other taxes, such as sales tax, or permitting fees, have to be raised to make up for lost revenue (Ginsberg, 1997: 34). The latter taxes are considered regressive taxes because lower income residents tend to pay a higher percentage of their overall income toward these taxes. As a result, while most residents despise property taxes, these taxes are one of the fairest ways to generate income for a local government.

A number of municipalities (and school districts) have introduced an earned income tax in addition to property taxes. Such a tax is levied upon anyone living or working in the municipality, such as those renting apartments as well as property owners. Proponents of such a tax argue that it spreads the tax burden to more people, and reduces the push back officials get from property owners in town. Senior citizens prefer this tax because it only assesses "earned" income received through employment. Income from social security, pensions, dividends and interest is not subject to this tax. Moreover, some residents may be required to pay an earned income tax where they work; if an earned income tax was then enacted where they reside, those residents would not be subjected to an additional tax. Most likely, the tax they already pay would simply go to their place of residence. The municipality where they work would lose the revenue, but the taxpayer in this case will be paying the same taxes as before.

Opponents of the earned income tax argue that some senior citizens may make more in a year from unearned income than some working families make from "earned" income, and it is therefore unfair for these working families to pay more than their fair share. Moreover, younger working families are more likely to have additional expenses associated with raising a family and, unlike many senior citizens, are also more likely to be paying the mortgages on their homes. However, even wealthy citizens who may have little earned income to show, and thus pay little earned income tax, must still pay property taxes on highly valued properties. To correct this problem, others support a personal income tax, which places a tax on all income, earned or unearned. Such a tax would include income from investments, pensions and social security as well as the traditional work-related sources of income. Such a tax would be a progressive tax, although politically a very difficult one for municipalities to pass and even more difficult to administer.

Another reason that there is opposition to the earned income tax is that local renters and those working in the municipality would also be subject to this tax. This could have consequences for the municipality. Local landlords and business owners could be less competitive in finding potential renters or employees if neighboring towns do not have this tax. Moreover, renters and wage earners working in the town may be earning less income than the residents who are homeowners in the municipality, and while the amount of taxes they would pay would be less in monetary terms, the impact this tax would have on lower income earners would be more severe. Gaffney has demonstrated that property ownership is, in the end, more concentrated than income and the property tax may be among the most progressive forms of taxation (1971: 411–412; see also Aaron, 1974: 212–221).

The system of taxing property is not without its problems. Properties of relatively comparable value may have disparate assessments and consequently the amount owners pay in property taxes can vary. As early as 1890, Seligman noted "it is a notorious fact that in scarcely two contiguous counties is the property—even real estate—appraised in the same manner or at the same rate" (Seligman, 1890: 25). Assessed values can theoretically fluctuate with undulations in the real estate market, creating additional disparities and affecting the amount of revenue a local government receives. Moreover, the property tax differs by jurisdiction, so that there may be inequities from one area to another. Affluent areas, with more expensive properties, will generate more revenue than more moderate areas, and residents of more affluent areas benefit from better schools and expanded services. These problems demonstrate that while there is some merit in relying on property taxes as a major source of income for municipalities, towns should not ignore needed reforms that help ensure fair property assessment. The property tax structure supports public education and leads to discrepancies in the quality of public school districts (Kozol, 1991: 54–57; Fernandez and Rogerson, 1996: 135–164).

Revenue generated from traffic violations is another source of additional funds municipalities rely on. Often small towns are accused of using the police as a revenue stream to plug holes in their budgets. A brief defense is in order. Historically, many small towns were once major hubs of activity surrounded by farmland. However, with suburban sprawl in the post–World War II period, development surrounding these small towns and neighboring suburbs clearly outpaced population growth and economic activity in the towns themselves. Even more recently developed areas encounter "drive through" traffic, as traffic is a regular feature of small town and suburban areas. As a result, people today are more likely to drive through such towns on their way to other destinations. At the same time, there is a tendency for people to rush more these days, with little regard for the residential character of the towns they are passing through. In other words, drivers generally exceed the speed limit and roll through stop signs, trying to get to their destination as quickly as possible. These traffic patterns conflict with one of the advantages of living in a small town: residents can walk to stores, parks, and restaurants. Impatient drivers threaten pedestrian safety. In addition to children, older small towns may have a large number of senior citizens and physically disabled residents. Traffic enforcement is needed to protect the safety of residents. Revenue generated from traffic enforcement is included in the budget. Indeed, the fears out of town drivers have about police in small towns may act as a deterrent to unsafe driving behavior that can pose a potential hazard to residents.

Public discussion with law enforcement officials about a possible increase in traffic enforcement vigilance as a means to generate revenues is illegal; however, that does not mean such conversations are never had. Moreover, the police department might decide on its own to increase enforcement in order to generate additional revenue for the purpose of requesting more personnel or equipment, and the increased revenue might have a psychological—if not budgetary—impact on the decision to honor that request. Small-town public officials can be seduced by the idea of using traffic enforcement as a means to raise revenue. After all, most of the people getting tickets are from outside the town. Having those outside the municipality subsidize the town's budget can be seen as a more attractive alternative than going to residents and asking for a tax increase!

While the temptation to increase traffic enforcement for revenue enhancement is always possible, there are strong moral reasons not to pursue this path. Often those who receive violations are the ones least able to pay for their tickets. Young drivers caught speeding are one such group. While they may be guilty of various traffic violations, the fines young drivers have to pay take up a disproportionate percentage of their overall income when compared to adult drivers. Racial bias in enforcing traffic laws has also been established (Feagin and Sikes, 1994: 199–202; Loury, 2015: 14–18; Chalabi, 2015). Such profiling does not necessarily mean that traffic laws are not violated, but their enforcement can have an institutional bias toward minority groups who lack the economic and political power to protest this bias.

Low-income working-class drivers get pulled over for a number of reasons, including not having an up to date registration or an expired inspection sticker. They are in violation because renewing their registration takes a big bite out of their monthly budget. They are caught in a vicious cycle. They are trying to work in order to keep afloat, but because of their low wages, they continue to struggle to make ends meet. They need a car to hold onto the job they have, but when faced with competing demands for their limited resources, renewing a vehicle's registration may be a lower priority than food and health-related costs. Why are low income drivers pulled over? Perhaps, again, it is because these groups lack economic and political power. Groups that lack economic and political power may feel intimidated to challenge this pattern, or may lack the wherewithal and confidence to make a public issue over it.

The idea of a balanced budget primarily refers to the general fund within the local government. The general fund is unrestricted money that can be used for any purpose deemed appropriate by local officials (Freeman, Shoulders and Allison, 2006: 113). The general fund is what pays most everyday expenditures, including payroll, insurance costs and business supplies. There are other funds that governments use for more restricted use. These funds may be come from state government or other sources, such as grants. The money in these funds can only be used for the intended purposes associated with that funding source. An example could be a fund from the state government that is intended for maintaining roads. Another could be a grant intended to preserve open space. A key principle of the Government Accounting Standards Board is that governments should be organized and operated on a fund basis (Freeman, Shoulders and Allison, 2006: 41). These standards are considered the "best practices" for government budgeting. For example, there is a "liquid fuels fund." In Pennsylvania, money from this fund comes from the state government and the size of the fund is determined by the number of roads in a municipality. Money from this fund can only be used for street-related expenses. This can include street repaving, engineering costs associated with road repairs, snow removal and assorted other "creative" street-related activities. Because this fund comes from the state, it is independently audited on an annual basis to insure that funds are indeed spent on their restricted use.

There are also funds that are created by local government as a way to reserve money for certain projects. These funds allow local governments to save money for a long-term need, or simply to budget money more efficiently. The source of money for these funds comes from the local government (i.e., from taxes, fees or traffic fines) and thus does not face some of the aforementioned restrictions. For example, a "Building Fund" can be created to set aside money that is to be used on the maintenance or expansion of municipal buildings. Funds of this type are transferred from the general fund. A fund for the police department would be another example. The yearly contribution to this fund from the general fund would constitute the police budget for the year. Another fund might be established in order to save money to purchase trucks, police vehicles or expensive equipment. A "Capital Projects Fund" might be created to cover large one-time expenditures for the town, such as equipment for a playground. A "Solid Waste Fund" could cover the cost of contracts the municipality has with trash haulers, and other expenses related to the removal of trash.

Because these kinds of funds come from general revenue sources, they do not have legal restrictions imposed on them. When budgeting, government officials can put any amount into these special funds. And when the local government is facing lean times, the amount of money allocated to these funds can be reduced.

The maintenance of infrastructural obligations, such as replacing a roof on a building, can be "deferred" for another year. "Deferred maintenance" is a way of utilizing government resources, especially when raising revenues through taxes is not a viable option. In the end, the consequential costs may be higher because of such delays. However, a different group of elected officials may be left needing to address the problem later on. Rosabeth Kantor has studied the problems of the crumbling infrastructure in the United States (2015: 1–26). While delaying maintenance can be an effective budgetary strategy for a given year or two, the use of "deferred maintenance" as a way to save government money (and not raise taxes on citizens for additional revenues) may lead to costlier expenses in the future.

These quasi-restricted types of funds have interesting implications for budgeting. Since the amount of annual contribution to these funds can vary from year to year, they also impact the overall health of the budget (i.e., the general fund). As previously noted, yearly contributions to these funds can be reduced to reflect leaner times; however, increasing the amount of money to these special funds can also make the general fund appear to have less money for other discretionary uses. In other words, a local government can store, or even hide money in these funds in order to create a hidden surplus to cover unexpected contingencies, such as a need for more police coverage or snow removal due to more snow storms. It also could be a way to give the impression that there is less government money to be used for purposes advocated by special interest groups within the municipality. Hiding a surplus not only stashes away money to be used for emergencies, but it also can become a strategic way to defend decisions not to give meaningful raises to employees, or to spend money on certain types of projects advocated for by some officials or residents. Thus, budgeting is as much a political process as well as a way to spend government money efficiently.

Most municipalities will discuss and approve a treasurer's report. The purpose of the treasurer's report is to provide elected officials and residents with an opportunity to oversee the stream of revenues and expenditures and to assess the financial state of the municipality. The level of careful scrutiny given by elected officials is difficult to know; the data can be very detailed and often there is little time given for review before a vote to approve the report. Members of council may receive the treasurer's report only at the night of the meeting, along with minutes of the previous meeting and other voluminous reports. Because all members of council in small towns are volunteers who serve while holding full-time jobs, many, if not all, never really have time to carefully review all the documents in front of them. Even when they are mailed to officials a week before the meeting, there is no guarantee that reports are carefully reviewed. Since both the minutes of the previous meeting and the treasurer's report are approved at the beginning of each meeting, they can be approved with little review. It is easy to trust that "someone else" has carefully reviewed the documents.

Many governments at all levels face financial crises. The local level of government is no exception, and can occur quickly. On the one hand, failure to recognize an impending financial crisis, or budgetary shortfall of funds, is understandable given that money from various sources—restricted or unrestricted—is added to the general fund for budgetary reasons. For example, grants received for specific projects are often added to the general fund. Although restricted for specific purposes, lumping grant money into the general fund may give the false illusion that there is sufficient money in the general fund. On the other hand, the downward trend in the financial health of a town should be discernible and the amount of grant money was not considerable. There should have been no illusion that all was well, although it might make someone feel that at least next week's payroll could be met!

Towns can institute the practice of keeping separate general fund money from grants, giving everyone a better sense of how much real money is available for use in the treasury. The practice of delaying payment or transfer of money allocated for community events such as parades during holidays, contributions to local nonprofit organizations and even one's own government funds (e.g., Building Fund) can be used to give the illusion that all is well. Spent money can be allowed to remain on the balance sheet, leaving the impression that there is more money than there really is. The practice of paying one's internal and external commitments early in the fiscal year can help avoid such potential problems.

A month or so after becoming council president, I was informed by the bookkeeper that there was no longer any money in the general fund to cover subsequent payrolls until new tax revenue was received in several months. In other words, the municipality was out of money to pay employees, including the police. Unless, the town came up with money somehow, it would be in default. A loan could be taken out, but while that would cover the immediate need of meeting payroll, the payments of the loan would then need to be added to the following year's budget. If the town ran out of money before taking the loan payments into account, adding those payments only serves to make the problem worse in the following year. Raising taxes was an even less desirable option.

We quickly embarked on a review of borough expenditures for the previous few months. This was done to determine if there were other sources of revenue that might be available for use, particularly in funds with restricted uses. If money from these funds could be used temporarily for general fund purposes, the budget crisis could be resolved. For example, while the solid waste fund was used primarily to pay the monthly bill from the trash hauler to cover the costs of garbage collection from the homes of residents, it also was noted that a couple of times, the solid waste fund had been used to cover the cost of dumping trash at the local landfill. While the fund was used to pay the monthly bill from the trash hauler to cover the costs of collecting garbage from homes of residents, it had also been used to cover the landfill bills for dumping garbage collected at trash receptacles in the park and from sweeping borough streets. The wages of the Streets Department employee, however, had never been paid from the solid waste fund. Rather, these wages traditionally were paid out of the general fund. It raised the question of whether the wages of employees sweeping, collecting and disposing of municipal refuse could also be paid out of the more robust solid waste fund. Because such a decision has serious legal implications, the legality of such a strategy was discussed with an attorney for the Pennsylvania Association of Boroughs. He concurred that work associated with the collection of solid waste could be paid out of the solid waste fund, including benefits. After determining the percentage of time municipal employees dedicated to the collection of "collective community refuse," the bookkeeper was then directed to transfer the appropriate amount of money paid to wages and benefits for these employees from the solid waste fund into the general fund. Presto! The borough now showed a slight surplus for the year, and the immediate financial crisis had been averted. Thanks to the ability to tap into this fund, no loans or tax increases were needed to cover the shortfall. While not a complete cure for the town's financial crisis, the move did provide some breathing room.

The practice of using the solid waste fund traditionally covered under the general fund (payroll costs for street department employees) to pay a fairly large portion of the street department employees continues today. While it helped to avoid financial disaster, there are implications for the town and its taxpayers. In the case of the solid waste bill, it is sent to residents quarterly. It is separate from the tax bill that is sent once a year. Quarterly bills normally remain the same for three years, which reflects the length of the contract with the company selected by the borough to pick up trash. Just prior to the end of the third year, the town then asks for bids for trash pickup for the next three-year cycle. This process allows competing companies to bid for the contract, and for the town to select the lowest bidder. However, the costs for trash pick up continue to increase, so each successive three-year contract is always higher than the preceding one. Once the new three-year contract is awarded, the quarterly bills sent out to residents have to be adjusted to reflect these increases. At this point a modest amount can also be added to the bill to reflect the "collective solid waste" costs to the town, that is, money that can continue to be used to help pay for the streets department personnel.

Residents read about the increases to their solid waste bills in the newspaper and, ultimately, when they paid their new solid waste bill. Increases are attributed to the higher charges set by the trash hauling company. Residents are not in a position to sort out how much of the increase in the trash comes from an increase in money for the trash hauler and how much is now being used to cover the costs of street department personnel. In essence, Borough officials have raised these quarterly bills to help partially pay the wages of streets department employees without raising general taxes. In fact, anything that can remotely be included as a solid waste matter is often taken out of the solid waste fund. These "creative usages"—once paid out of the general fund—can now be shifted over for payment out of the solid waste fund. These increases in the solid waste bill (reflecting use of the fund to cover other costs) over and above the increase is really a hidden tax increase on borough residents. These increases pay for costs previously paid out of the general fund. The costs have simply been transferred to another bill that taxpayers have to pay. These increases are not seen as tax increases. And yet, they are tax increases by any other name.

Because residents are absorbing new costs that are outside the typical tax rate structure, [in this case from property taxes,] local officials confidently say that they are not raising taxes. Indeed, raising taxes is the bane of any politician as any cursory examination of campaign ads during elections demonstrates. Finding indirect ways to raise government revenues from residents allows politicians to assert that they do not raise taxes. Indeed, every year, when the borough passes its budget, and the millage rate remains the same as it has for the previous year, the newspaper headline after the meeting always reads "No Tax Increase Again for the Town." The article usually would include a quote from a council member stressing how hard council worked to keep costs down. It likely fails to mention the fact that at a previous meeting, the solid waste bill was increased to cover expenses previously paid out of the general fund that are now being paid for by the solid waste fund.

"Tax increases by any other name" can take other forms as well. Many a president of the United States has cut taxes and ran for re-election on the merits of that action. To pay for those tax cuts, however, social programs may have been cut. Others then have to bear the cost of those cuts, such as those who were receiving the benefits or another entity such as the local or the state government or a nonprofit organization. If less money is subsequently given to individual states, these states then have to deal with less revenues in their budgets. At the same time, the governors of these states likely also run for office promising either tax cuts or no new tax increases. A proposed tax increase would only assure defeat in the next election. At the same time, the costs of state government have increased. To compensate for the loss of revenue and increased costs, state governments then must raise fees wherever possible (for inspections, licenses, etc.) or reduce payments to local school districts. This, in turn, forces school districts to raise property taxes. The bulk of property taxes in suburban towns go to the school district, and that part has only increased over time, due in part to the relative reduction in the revenue stream from the state. Battles over whether to increase or maintain taxes take place at the school board level. School board officials (and local governments) are located at the bottom of this funding chain. They have no one else to pass costs on to, except tax payers themselves (Dye and Reschovsky, 2008; Wu, 2009: 80–84). Despite calls for tax cuts and no new tax increases, everyone has been paying more overall. Maintaining taxes at one level of government often means that lower levels of government have to bear more costs.

Another way local governments transfer costs to residents without raising taxes is through the sale of assets, such as a sewer authority. For example, almost every municipality has or had its own sewer authority. Eventually the burden of maintaining and upgrading aging sewer systems overwhelmed many municipalities and the county or private companies started buying the local sewer systems. While centralization of the sewer system makes sense, each municipality negotiates the sale of its own system. The outcome of these sales varies.

In our town, when the sewer authority was transferred to the county, elected officials decided to take no additional cash for the system, and instead chose to have the county freeze sewer bills of residents for fifteen years. Any increases after fifteen years had to be gradual and not exceed a certain percentage. The rationale behind this approach was to protect residents from rate increases as long as possible, since the costs of maintaining and upgrading the aging sewer system would only increase over time. Residents would thus be spared from having to absorb these increased costs for a period of time. However, any additional money associated with a "no strings attached" transfer was not given to the town.

Other municipalities might have chosen a different tact. They might accept large cash settlements as part of the sale, which would increase the town's coffers. Rate hike protections given for residents would be either eliminated or confined to a three-year period. The lack of rate protection in the transfer would be the trade off for the cash. Residents in these towns would soon receive hefty sewer bill increases once the limited rate freeze was over. When the higher bills arrive in the mail, any anger would need to be directed toward the County Sewer Authority, not toward the local municipality that negotiated the terms of the sale. The municipality took the cash, and passed the cost of that decision through a third party to residents. This is one more case of a hidden tax increase by another name.

Another way residents are charged more without calling it a tax is through the permitting process for various activities. For example, if someone wants to build an addition to their home, remodel a kitchen or a bathroom, or replace a front porch, a building permit is required. The building inspector for the municipality then inspects the project at different times to make sure everything conforms to building codes. The expertise of the building inspector insures that the resident is protected from unsafe work, and the local government is protected from having to deal with the consequences of unsafe work in the future. While the building inspector could be paid out of general revenues for services rendered, most small municipalities charge the resident for the building permit. Some larger municipalities provide enough business for the building inspector, or a staff of inspectors, to make the job a full-time salaried position. In small towns, however, there is not enough work, and building inspectors are often hired on a part-time basis. One payment model is that they receive 70% of the building permit and the municipality keeps the remaining 30% to cover administrative costs. Such a permit is in effect a tax increase. Raising permit fees increases what the building inspector receives, but it also increases the government's revenues. This is not to suggest that having a building inspector enforce safety codes is not an important practice; it can help prevent fires and heads off problems down the road. However, such an arrangement becomes another way for local governments to take in additional revenue without having to officially raise taxes.

Some argue that costs such as home inspections should be borne by residents using these services. The concern is why should other residents subsidize a building inspector's time inspecting private residences. A similar argument can be made for fire inspections. While there is merit to this argument, one could argue as well that such services should be taken out of general funds. Everyone at some point is likely to need these services in one form or another. In fact, many services targeted at individual residents are already paid out of general revenues. For example, the police are not called to everyone's homes, and yet the costs of the police department are paid out of general funds. Not everyone uses the playgrounds in town, but all residents bear the cost for them. There may be some merit to this "pay for use" argument as well, but as long as a permit can be charged, the local government generates revenue and the cost is transferred to those specifically using the service.

In addition towns can create new forms of taxes that are paid by those outside the municipality. For example, some big cities pass a wage tax that requires those who live outside the municipality but who work inside its borders to pay a certain percentage of their wages or salaries back to the municipality. These cities argue that they maintain the roads and provide security, among other things for nontax payers who use these services on a regular basis, so they require nontax payers to contribute to these benefits. Cities can afford to implement such a tax because most of those working in the cities are unlikely to quit their jobs and find employment elsewhere. Jobs in cities, especially professional jobs, usually pay more because the cost of living in cities is generally higher. Smaller towns cannot necessarily afford to pass such a tax because it would make the town less competitive for small businesses and even apartment dwellers. When most local jobs are in the service sector and similar ones can be found in neighboring municipalities without such taxes, it is presumed that people will chose to work in these other municipalities to avoid paying such taxes. If there is a labor shortage for workers in these lower paid jobs, then a town with such a tax might have to offer a higher wage to be attractive to prospective employees. Wage taxes are therefore less of an option for small towns unless such taxes are shared by a larger contiguous area.

Another strategy towns can use to shift the burden of increasing revenues from nonresidents is through an amusement tax. Such a tax can be levied when there happens to be a golf course or an amusement park in a municipal area. Even bars that have video games are subject to this tax. Such taxes are implemented in towns and municipalities around the country with amusement parks. While the proprietors of the amusement oppose such a tax, it is paid by the consumer (who pays an additional cost of attendance), not the company itself. Moreover, because most municipalities that have amusements pass such a tax, companies cannot argue that they are in an unfair competitive position because of the tax. This is a bona fide tax increase, but since it is not levied on residents of the town, it is one of the more popular tax increases that a politician can enact! There are plenty of similar taxes that can be used to generate additional revenue. Parking meters in a shopping area work like this. A hotel tax for visitors is another example. These are equivalent to tax increases levied on a public who probably does not live in the area and thus lacks the power to protest, other than avoiding the town or the golf course. Yet, these approaches for generating tax revenue are used everywhere. They are hard to avoid, regardless of where you go. While the amount levied on any given individual is not great enough to deter most people, the total amount of revenue generated for the municipality can be considerable.

Today, most towns are facing financial difficulties, and any source of revenue enhancement needs to be explored. However, these financial difficulties do not exist in a political vacuum. Residents may be sympathetic to budgetary woes facing the town; still any tax increase imposed is viewed unfavorably. Disguised taxes, such as an increased solid waste bill are not easily viewed by residents as tax increases. But increases in property taxes are clearly understood by residents in the town, thus provoking discontent and politicians who propose them are likely to feel their wrath. Therefore, raising revenues by taxing others is always a preferable option when possible, as such a scenario makes elected politicians more popular among constituents.

During lean budgetary years, when money is especially tight, the general fund should be seen as a 'last resort" for making expenditures. Expenditures should be made from other funds whenever possible, for example, payment for a building or garage from the building fund and minor street repairs out of the streets fund. While taking payments out of these funds is legal, it is often considered more prudent to reserve these funds for big-ticket items like renovations, replacement of a boiler or street resurfacing. If money is taken out of these funds too regularly, then it can be a problem when money is suddenly needed for big-ticket items, as the previous discussion of our crumbing infrastructure noted.

When there is a financial shortfall in the general fund it can be very tempting to "raid" these funds, though continued use of this practice could lead to the depletion of the funds, requiring a more systematic examination of the finances of the town. Many a tax increase has been levied on the public because these funds were "raided" too often and then the costs of unexpected projects necessitated a substantial tax increase. Many towns or school districts have raided such funds only to then need to raise taxes later. Newly elected officials can find themselves with no other choice because of the short-sighted actions of their predecessors (sometimes called "kicking the can down the road"). Of course, one could argue that such raiding practices merely delay eventual tax increases that have been forestalled by use of other funds.

Sometimes raiding funds is done in anticipation of increased revenues, such as the opening of new businesses that would provide additional mercantile taxes, or signs of the end of a recession that will lead to more sales of homes and concomitant transfer taxes. Raiding funds, however, could also be used to pay for projects or new employees, for example, which was really beyond the scope of what the municipality should have been taking on in the first place. Sometimes, instead of saying no to such requests, it is easier to say yes and then pay for it by "creative" accounting schemes. However, as the singer-songwriter Dar Williams says in her song, *As Cool As I Am*, "the truth is just like time, it catches up and it just keeps going." It is only a matter of time before the consequences of such financial folly wreak havoc on the ability of elected official to run the town effectively. Elected officials could be hoping they will be out of office by the time reality sets in, when the proverbial piper needs to be paid—leaving the problem to newly elected officials. Let them be the ones to raise taxes! Many a governor, mayor or council has inherited such a financial crisis.

As noted above, these practices also lead to deferred maintenance of the infrastructure of towns, such as roads, buildings, bridges, etc. as short-term budgetary needs become a priority over infrastructural matters, whose problems may take some time to become evident. However, deferring maintenance eventually raises the price tag for fixing problems as small problems become bigger problems over time.

A sensible way to avoid a financial crisis is to put both allocated and required/expected expenditures into the various funds (e.g., building fund, truck fund) on the first month of the year and then pay ordinary expenses out of the general fund. Town support for local community agencies in the area (American Legion Posts, Emergency Services/Ambulance organization, garden clubs) also are allocated early in the fiscal year. The advantages to such an approach are several. First, by paying out the money to the funds in January, the money left in the general fund is unrestricted. This practice allows officials to more clearly track the amount of money really available for general use. What you see is what you really have. Second, if these payments are made and it is still possible to pay for regular expenditures out of the general fund, then the restricted funds can grow (with interest). The money in these funds would be there for major expenses. A government in a healthy financial situation should be able to handle the budget this way. A backup plan, when the financial picture is weaker, is to hold off making these obligatory payments to the restricted funds until the tax money comes in. A local government, however, should not have to resort to this practice if its financial state is solid.

Even residents not well versed in reading budgets can still get a sense of the financial health of their municipality. Treasurer reports have to be approved once a month and they must be made available to the public. If copies are not handed out at meetings, a copy should be made available for the public to review in the municipal office. Although the internet is not accessible to everyone, the internet could also be another effective way of making public documents available to the public. Examining them over time will show where money has been taken out and whether funds are growing or being depleted. A comparison of the same months' Treasurer Reports over several years, such as the month of January and September should provide a good picture of the financial health of the municipality. One can look at the balance of the general fund as well as other funds, such as the building fund, and see if the amounts have increased, decreased, or remained the same over time. Did a decline of money in funds designated for capital improvements take place without a corresponding increase in meaningful capital improvements? If not, these funds may have been raided to cover routine costs and avoid raising taxes.

Another problem government officials have to contend with is the "budget mentality" of those appointed officials who are responsible for budgets but who at the same time have little control over the size of that budget. More often than not, those responsible for managing budgets always feel more money should be allocated to them. This mentality is common in all bureaucracies, including government, business, nonprofits and even higher education. This mentality fosters a desire to spend all allocated money whether or not it needs to be spent each year. This thinking is inspired by several factors. First, the money is there to be spent. Allocated money is not viewed as one's personal money. It is easier to spend someone else's money. Second, many feel that if allocated money is not spent, those with the power to shape the budget may decide that next year less money is really needed and subsequent allocations will be reduced. This may indeed be the case in some workplaces, but even where it is not true distrust of those who make budgetary allocations higher up makes one act as if it was true.

Everyone benefits when towns spend what they really need and not the full budgeted amount. If those in charge of budgets spent less than their allocated amounts, elected officials in charge of the overall budget and the public would more likely be supportive of requests for additional money when specific needs arise. Such a model might imply greater trust all around. It would likely save taxpayer money in the long run, and money that should be spent on important items would get covered. However, trust that such a process would occur usually does not exist and that distrust is a two-way street. The ones with the power to control budget allocations do not necessarily trust their personnel to use allocated money as efficiently as possible and those in charge of budgets think their higher-ups are always trying to shortchange them. Reconciling this problem is not easy. One idea might be to allow those in charge of budgets the ability to bank a certain percentage of the money that is saved from their allocation. For example, if half the savings now became unrestricted "mad money" for the budget manager, there would be some incentive for the manager to save. The overall municipality would also benefit from its share of the savings as well. This kind of policy could become an accounting nightmare, and may indeed conflict with regulations regarding nonprofit organizations, but these are ultimately technical obstacles that could be overcome if there was a will to move in this direction.

Another "budget mentality" often observed is that so many people, whether employees or paid professionals with whom local governments contract for services, assume that any form of government has deep pockets with money to spend. They often believe that government officials cry poverty as a way to save money, either for their own pet projects or just to save money for money's sake.

An addition to our municipal building was needed in order to house new fire trucks that the fire company was acquiring. A local architect generously offered his services sufficiently below what other bidders proposed and began to draw up plans. He was told that the town had only $100,000 to spend on the addition, which was the amount of financing and grants that was secured. The architect interviewed everyone, from council members, the police department, the borough secretary, and the fire company officials, among others, to learn what each of these various constituencies needed in the new facility. They were trying to include everyone's wishes in their plans. Every meeting they were reminded that the town had to remain firm on the $100,000 limit. The night the council met to approve the specs for advertising for bids from builders, council members were informed that the latest calculations indicated that the addition would cost much more than anticipated. It was not clear why the increased projection of costs was only made available the evening of the meeting. After a long discussion during the meeting itself, we made the decision to advertise the specs anyway. The specs were already written and paid for, leaving little to lose. There was a long-shot hope that the town would be lucky. The lowest bid was $279,000 (more than double what had originally been quoted). Council rejected all bids. The architect was then asked to make a new bare bones design for the building. The lowest bid for the scaled back building was $129,000, still over what was available. With last minute additional financial support from a local state legislator and the fire company, the additional funds were secured and construction began. Paid professionals—architects in this case—who offered their services at a reduced rate, and did a great job designing the building, still seemed to assume there was a way for the local government to find the extra money for the enhanced building design. There is an ongoing belief that a local government has more money than government officials let on, and since it is not anyone's personal money, more money can be found and spent. However, especially in lean financial times when residents are particularly wary of any tax increase, elected officials have to stay firm.

Sometimes projects end up costing more money because overruns or unanticipated problems emerge once the project is underway. Professionals, such as engineers, who are hired by the town, are expected to monitor requests for additional funds as a way to keep such increased costs under control.

CONCLUSION

Governmental budgets, whether at the local, county, state or federal levels, are a way of collecting and spending the public's money as efficiently as possible. Careful budgeting certainly allows for that efficiency. It is, however, clear that the budget is also a political document. Priorities are established, and the expenditures of revenues are allocated in line with these priorities.

Requiring a balanced budget makes sense because it forces elected officials to exercise financial discipline. They are forced to stay within their means. Shortfalls, however, can emerge due to unexpected costs, such as a higher incidence of weather-related problems. Once government officials start planning budgets that hide surpluses to insure that unanticipated expenses can be covered, the idea of a balanced budget becomes an exercise more than a reality. It helps set goals with which to insure financial discipline and to reduce wasteful spending.

The political climate that fosters an antitax culture may cause elected officials to engage in creative ways to tax the public ("by any other name"). Such practices, while effective in the short term, do not increase transparency in government. Moreover, this culture tends to encourage deferred maintenance that can lead to higher prices in the future.

Ways to raise government revenues outside the traditional route of raising property taxes are often considered. Ways that tax increases can be masked help elected officials in a political environment that is anathema to raising taxes. Residents, however, still end up paying to cover what are essentially "tax increases by any other names."

It is a difficult, but not impossible, task to monitor public documents in order to ascertain how much money a given municipality has and what is sufficient to run the government. Such review will uncover whether funds will likely fall and require additional revenues (e.g., tax increases), or whether the municipality is holding on to too much money that could be used to reduce taxes. The general fund is where most people look to determine the financial health of a government. However, money can be moved to other funds to give the "appearance" of a shortfall, keeping available money hidden. As noted above, there are ways to examine the governmental budgets to ascertain if such creative moves are at work. Questioning elected officials about the use of all funds besides the general fund is also useful.

Chapter 2

Political Conflict at the Local Level

Government, whether at the federal, state or local level, is entrusted with the responsibility of making laws and policies that naturally have an impact on all individuals within its borders. As a federally based government system, the Tenth Amendment to the Constitution gives states the right to enact laws that are not prohibited to them. Just as the federal government determines the context for how individual states can act, state governments set the structure of local governments as well as the parameters by which they can make laws. Given that each state can set different rules regarding what local governments can and cannot do, the forms of local government may vary on what they can do from state to state. Even within a state, there can be variations. In addition to the budgeting process already discussed, there are common threads to what local governments can do across the country. They pass laws, or ordinances, that govern.

Although everyone is affected by the way government acts, it should not be assumed that everyone benefits equally from its actions, or that everyone even receives some benefits at all. In fact some, if not many, could lose out from government policies. It would make more sense to assume that there are usually winners and losers in just about everything that government does. As a result, people, through their organizations, unions, religious institutions and political parties get involved in trying to influence government to work on behalf of their interests and beliefs, even if actions they are supporting go against the interests and beliefs of others. Hence, conflicts that take place within the political arena usually lead to winners and losers.

On the national, or federal, level, the main forces usually take the form of competing social classes, particularly between the business sector and the working class (Truchil, 1988: 91–126; Domhoff, 2010: 1–23). For example, issues over raising the minimum wage or facilitating the exporting of manufacturing jobs overseas leave business interests at odds with those of labor in the United States, particularly in the manufacturing sector. Businesses gain by being able to keep wages low or by moving to areas whether within the country or overseas to hire workers who will work for less. Businesses may increase profits from such actions, and workers may have a reduced standard of living or lose jobs altogether because of these actions.

How taxes are raised or cut also take class politics into account as well. Different groups can benefit or lose from having to pay more or less in taxes and/or certain types of taxes such as capital gains or a sales tax. This is not to say that politics at the national level is always defined in strict class terms. Issues such as abortion and capital punishment take on other social contexts, such as gender and religion. Moreover, conflicts also occur between different sectors within business, such as businesses that compete globally and those more confined to the United States, or labor communities, such as skilled/educated labor and unskilled labor. However, most issues at the national level can be seen as shaped by social class, and class-based organizations such as business-based organizations and labor unions take very active roles at the national level, even if the resources they bring to bear in their roles are very unequal.

Politics at the local municipal or county level are often shaped by coalitions of combatants than differ from those at the national level. Different coalitions of elected officials, regardless of political party affiliation, can have differences over whether to raise, reduce or maintain taxes, and where to tax. And elected officials have their pet projects or individual preferences, for example, renovating playgrounds and parks, hiring more police or other municipal workers, or purchasing newer trucks and equipment, among others. So there are many areas where government officials can disagree, most of which are not covered in the media or even known by most residents.

If Karl Marx wrote that a specter haunts society by it splitting into two major camps, namely capitalists and the working class, a different specter haunts society at the local municipal level (Marx, 1972: 331–362). In their pivotal work, Logan and Molotch found that there are two main groups or combatants at the local level who are organized over the issue of development, or the intensification of land use within the municipality (Logan and Molotch, 1987: 2–4). One group can be called the "growth machine" and this group seeks to intensify land use or growth within a given area. The other group is largely made up of residents and environmental groups who seek to defend the integrity of their communities and local environments and oppose many of the development plans proposed by the growth machine. Intensifying land use basically means that existing space, or land becomes denser through building of homes, apartment buildings, shopping centers, or any other type of development that brings more people and businesses to the area. In the process, economic development is accelerated.

The conflict over land use suggests that politics at the local level of government has its own distinct dynamic that is different from national politics, with different sets of alliances and coalitions. This reality, however, does not preclude the fact that local areas are also greatly influenced by the consequences of national policies. Of course they are! For example, policies that encourage the exporting of jobs overseas can create unique unemployment problems for a given local area if major employers leave that area. Fiscal crises then follow because local governments have to face the reality of fewer taxpayers, in the form of both companies and employed workers as well as more individuals subsequently calling on government for social services. As noted in the previous chapter, when federal and state governments choose not to raise taxes, or even cut taxes, and subsequently cut back on spending, increased pressure is placed on local governments to make up for these cuts in spending. The nature of political conflicts may have evolved over time and become more complex, but the battle lines have remained. Nevertheless, the conflict that takes place between proponents of increased growth or development, on the one hand, and local residents, on the other, are more unique to local levels of government, and it is this conflict as well as the role that local government plays in mediating this conflict is the focus of this chapter.

BASIS FOR THE GROWTH MACHINE

Much discussion of the growth machine focuses on the urban setting as the unit of analysis, rather than suburban areas or small towns (Logan and Molotch, 1987; 50–98). Nonetheless, it still applies, maybe even more so, to suburban areas and the small towns within these suburban areas (Beauregard, 2006: 70–100; Jackson, 1985: 231–245). The flight of capital and residents from cities to suburban areas since the end of World War II has long been established. The federal government indeed helped to set the foundation for the movement to the suburbs after the war. The resources the federal government spent on building interstate highways and water and sewage expansion, allowing tax deductions on mortgages, providing lower mortgage rates and a home mortgage insurance program through the Federal Housing Authority, established the conditions for the growth of suburbs and small towns, to the detriment of urban areas (Beauregard, 2001: 129–138; Duany, et al., 2000: 7–8). It should be noted, however, that others see the post–World War II growth in suburbs as different in scale, but not qualitatively distinct from previous trends of suburbanization (Bruegmann, 2005: 43). Nonetheless, the growth of the suburbs and small towns after World War II was significant, and it has affected the political landscape in these areas.

Demographic trends in the 1970s and 1980s also fueled suburban and small-town development. The coming of age of baby boomers, who began to start families of their own, signaled a new demand for housing (Bruegmann, 2005: 60). Many corporations increasingly moved their administrative headquarters to suburban areas because of cheaper real estate costs, lower taxes and greater geographical proximity to their relocated employees. Indeed, development of the "Route 1 Corridor" in New Jersey and Bucks County, PA, "Silicon Valley" at California or the Route 128 Corridor in the Boston area emerged in the late 1970s and 1980s reflect this trend.

What Beauregard calls "frontier capitalism" where households left the cities for the suburban areas, then created space for new immigrants in urban areas (Beauregard, 2006: 90–92). Suburban and small-town growth was tied to housing that was made more affordable. Many urban residents chose to make the move out of the city as the suburbs were seen as a good value, helping satisfy a need for privacy and personal space with which one can control though landscaping, etc. (Martinson, 2000: 54). Businesses also relocated to these newly developed areas to meet consumption needs of these relocated groups who left the city. Suburban areas became contained entities within themselves; most people hardly went into large cities anymore, except for the occasional special event, such as going to a museum, sporting event, or a special restaurant. People lived their lives within the suburbs and small towns—working, shopping and dining there. Local governments in these areas had to grow as well to provide essential services. They became dependent on "own-source" revenues such as real estate taxes to fund the costs of government. If an area was to grow and have services to attract and accommodate that growth, local government officials would see growth or the intensification of land use as a way to expand the tax base. As a result, growth was a necessary by-product of this post–World War II phenomenon.

Many writers, as noted above, have attributed the rise of suburban areas to these trends. Private businesses emerged within these areas to take advantage of the opportunities growth created. Meeting consumer demands was a profitable business venture. Once entrenched in an area, continued growth becomes a *raison d'etre* for many of these businesses, especially businesses like developers whose profits dependent on continued intensification of land use. Organizing politically to influence local government policy to advance their economic interests by allowing conditions that promote growth simply becomes an extension of this process. Indeed, this basic reality behooves those dependent on the intensification of land use to be active politically, whether by contributing to political campaigns and joining local business-oriented organizations such as the rotaries and chambers of commerce or other similar organizations. The growth machine thus becomes an integral part of the political landscape.

Moreover, businesses that became part of the growth machine are generally fixed within a geographical area, including suburban areas, ones encompassing small towns, and stand to prosper from the intensification of land use. Given the relatively recent character of suburban development when compared to urbanization, there is usually considerable amounts of virgin territory (i.e., open space that is still undeveloped). While it might serve a greater social and environmental need to renovate existing buildings that are abandoned or in disrepair in urban areas, there is greater profit to be gained by private entrepreneurs in developing suburban areas. Clearly, tremendous economic growth and concomitant population increases have occurred in suburban areas surrounding cities. Thus, the concept of the growth machine is relevant for suburban as well as urban areas.

The nature of growth in suburbia may take different forms than in urban areas. For example, there may be less emphasis on attracting manufacturing/industrial development (although this type of growth has clearly occurred) and more emphasis on housing, real estate/commercial and office buildings. However, the processes of growth and the conflicts that follow are the same. Indeed, interest in growth has been called "the overriding commonality among important people in a given locale—at least insofar as they have any important local goals at all" (Molotch, 1974: 310). Any of these choices lead to intensification of land use. Conflicts between the growth machine, which wants to see further development, and residents, who want to protect the character of their community still takes a political dimension.

The desire of local leaders to increase growth is not a new phenomenon in US history. In the past, there were struggles, efforts and/or conspiracies over the construction and location of railroads, canals and other infrastructural projects (Kolko, 1965: 102–126). Indeed, it is imbedded in our historical tradition, as development and growth in the United States has been relatively unrestrained. In their study of the relationships between local governments, corporations and real estate interests in the United States, compared to Japan and Italy, Molotch and Vicari observed that the United States is "unusual in the degree to which regulation of property development is weak and decentralized. The United States is still extreme in the freedom given to entrepreneurs to manipulate the environment for profit" (Molotch and Vicari, 1988: 189). For advanced industrial societies, the United States has the least regulation of the environment. Coupled with the degree of autonomy enjoyed at the local level, local government decision-making becomes an important area for growth-oriented businesses to get involved.

The key to the concept of a growth machine is the idea that local companies and businesspeople are the principal participants in local politics. They are organized, active in the political arena and they work together to create a pro-growth agenda for the local area. Members of the growth machine tend to be active in various local-based organizations such as the Chamber of Commerce and Rotaries and consequently lend a pro-development point of view to these organizations. They also tend to contribute to the campaigns of those politicians sharing their vision at the state, county and local levels. They tend to extol the virtues of growth at public forums and use their influence in the political arena to ensure that their values become articulated in local government policy. They lobby state legislatures and county commissions so that pro-development policies prevail, weakening the ability of local governments to control growth in their areas. They use their influence to help assure the election or appointment of judges who are pro-growth or friendly to business, so that their chances for success in court increase when challenged by local municipalities. Or, that they can successfully overturn decisions made by local governments in their appeals in court.

There are additional ways that a value system is used to promote the goals of the growth machine. When the focus is on a territorial area, growth is depicted as a way to unite constituencies that might otherwise be divided. Divisions of race, class, gender and ethnicity, among others may find common ground by uniting people where they live and pay taxes (Cox, 1999: 22–23). Emphasizing a unifying theme such as expanding the tax base can be an issue all members of a community can rally around. Of course, threats from the potential impact of growth on the community can also be a unifying theme. These themes are reiterated through "civic boosterism" at meetings of the Chamber of Commerce or local rotary clubs—wherever the pro-growth ideology is promulgated (Short, 1999: 37–54).

The desire for growth also takes place within an economic and political context. Regions that have experienced capital flight in manufacturing or the loss of white collar jobs as large companies move their headquarters elsewhere may be under more pressure to embrace growth (Humphrey, 2001: 117–118). The types of growth that are proposed, such as efforts to increase manufacturing, commercial business or tourism also can be factors encouraging the establishment of coalitions whose goal is to intensify land use within a given area. Moreover, there is the goal of diversifying an area's tax base in order to reduce the burden on those who pay property tax (Schneider, 1992: 214). Adding growth, and thereby new taxpayers to the area, should presumably lower the taxes of those already in the area.

WHO MAKES UP THE GROWTH MACHINE?

Builders and Developers

Builders and developers are the *sine qua non* of the growth machine. Since their livelihood comes from intensifying land use by building new homes, office buildings and shopping centers, they can only naturally prosper from continuing to build and build. In other words, their economic survival requires greater intensification of land use, or increased growth. It is in their personal self-interest to promote growth.

As noted above, most developers tend to be local and are geographically fixed to a local area, usually a county or equivalent region. Some larger developers may have branches in multiple areas, even across several states, moving into what they consider to be high-growth areas. Their overall relationships, however, are with the local level. They must stay in their general area, which is why an atmosphere of continued growth is vital to their livelihood. They organize politically in order to promote the articulation of their interests in local government policy. Lubell, et al., found that developers are well organized and well financed and are capable of becoming "powerful articulators" of pro-development sentiments (Lubell, et al. 2005: 710–711). As such, they exert the necessary influence needed to translate their preferences into government policy.

Their influence has only become stronger since 1980, when the development industry underwent consolidations and mergers (Knox, 2008: 67). Previously, suburban development was dominated by smaller and medium-sized companies. Through consolidation developers achieve greater economies of scale and they are also better equipped to deal with opposition forces. Knox has called the local landscape a "developer's utopia" due to these trends (2008: 66–88).

Real Estate Companies and Brokers

The real estate industry does not construct buildings. Instead, they act as brokers for those buying and selling properties. Their commissions are thus based on the sale and resale of properties. Since the real estate industry earns income through commissions from the sale of properties, intensification of land use means more houses, office buildings and commercial properties to sell (and resell). As a consequence, the real estate industry is a *bona fide* member of the local growth machine.

Most real estate companies are locally based. Many have national names like ReMax and Coldwell Banker, but the franchises are locally owned and those who sell properties remain local. They tend to be very pro-growth in outlook and when well organized, can exert pressure on local government officials (Lubell, et al., 2008: 712). As an overarching value, they will support pro-growth views. They speak at local town meetings about the benefits of continued growth (the benefits and disadvantages of ongoing growth to an area will be discussed shortly). As with developers, continued growth is vital to their livelihood. Interestingly, while organized real estate interests are outspoken critics of policies that seek to preserve open space and protect the environment, they may nonetheless benefit from these policies if they result in higher housing prices that can be passed onto consumers (Lubell, et al., 2008: 724).

Utilities

Utilities include providers of electricity, water and even cable television. There has been increased deregulation of the utility industry, particularly for the electricity providers in various parts of the United States. This deregulation allows consumers to shop around and purchase electricity from different companies, and the company that originally was the sole source of power continues to generate the electricity.

Public utilities are very capital-intensive with considerable investments in gas lines, power and transmission infrastructures. As a result, most utility companies have a "local dependence resulting from the spatial immobility" of their investments (Cox and Mair, 1988: 308). That is, they are locally fixed in their general area. Even if large utility companies are national in scope, such as cable television providers, or if they cover very large areas, such as electricity providers, they generally have virtual control of their utility in their areas. Moreover, utility companies still get to charge all customers for use of the electricity lines, generation and other related costs, so that even when one switches to another electricity provider, approximately half of the monthly electricity bill remains with the local utility company.

Because utilities are generally tied to a given area, they too benefit from intensification of land use in order to acquire new customers and increase profits. Utility companies that also serve urban areas have been faced by the flight of industries and residents from those areas, as well as the subsequent loss of revenues from a declining customer base. Encouraging greater growth in suburban areas allows those utility companies to recoup those losses, and even surpass their previous customer base. As a consequence, utility companies tend to identify with the values of growth, and these values tend to dominate the business community as a whole as well as the agencies that regulate them (Maher, 1977: 173, 183).

Water companies are also utilities that seek intensification of land use. According to scholars who have researched water, they can only be fully understood within the context of the politics and economy of regional growth (Walker and Williams, 1982: 117). For developers and other members of the growth machine, the availability of water plays a very critical role as an infrastructural necessity for development. However, water is also known as a "common pool resource," a good that is accessible to everyone (nonexcludable) but can be subjected to overuse (see Krugman and Wells, 2015:

499–500). If one considers water companies as serving the public good, one has to also ask who decides what the public good is. And within a political context, the public good is associated with increased intensification of land use, and serving the needs of increased development. Water companies, like other utility companies, are an intrinsic member of the growth machine.

Politicians

Any discussion of a local growth machine must include the elected politicians who can make policy that can aid or impede growth in a given region. The larger the local municipality, the more money a candidate needs to wage a successful campaign. At a county level, it is even more critical. Those that benefit from greater intensification of land use tend to be big donors to political candidates (Logan and Molotch, 1987: 67). In other words, politicians who accept these donations to become "one of the boys" are, to a large extent, willing advocates for the growth machine. They may even benefit materially as well as politically from such a relationship. Moreover, politicians who tend to stand in the way of the growth machine are likely to lose their support and risk losing political influence—if not the next election. Because of this relationship, politicians are the key members of the growth machines.

The connection of politicians to the growth machine goes beyond the mere influence that donations may secure. Most municipalities tend to be dominated by one party, although there are some areas where there is no clear dominant political party, and there are cases where party strength in suburban areas shifts (Karp, 1973: 27–42; McKee and Teigen, 2009: 484–495). The dominant party thus tends to dominate elections, and for members of the growth machine, those in power are the ones with whom to show support. Nonetheless, there is no evidence that suggests Republican or Democratic elected officials are not willing to work with the growth machine (Sole-Olle and Viladecans-Marshal, 2013: 12–14). In other words, elected local officials of both major parties are willing to work with the growth machine.

The party in power (this also applies to Democratic strongholds in urban and suburban areas) tends to comprise a "political machine" that rewards ongoing support. This support by members of the growth machine includes political support in the form of canvassing, hosting meetings and parties for candidates, as well as the typical financial support. Since a party tends to benefit, members of the growth machine would choose to back the winning party, and they receive the benefits of patronage for their efforts. Party patronage can range from serving on Authorities and Boards (that regulate development!) to serving on the board of directors of the local community college to finding "public" jobs for loyal supporters or even summer jobs for their children. Especially at the town and county levels, where commissioners or freeholders can serve as both the executive and legislative branches of government, the same people are enacting policy and making political appointments. Those who get these appointments receive them with the understanding that they will remain loyal to the party that put them there. As one political operative in the county put it, "Employees are hired with the understanding that they will support the party. Clearly, party loyalty and support are an unspoken requirement" (*Daily Intelligencer/Montgomery Record*, September 23, 1983: 30).

Because of the role of party patronage, politicians have an additional reason to support growth-oriented projects. These projects provide patronage jobs as well as meet the interests of the growth machine. It becomes a basis for reciprocity where there are so many opportunities for elected officials to provide for those who have been loyal to the party. Indeed, it is common to see engineers and legal representation appointed to local government posts after they have shown previous political support or connectedness.

Engineers, Lawyers and other Professionals

Professionals such as engineers, architects, lawyers and surveyors, among others, stand to benefit from increased intensification of land use. Architects and surveyors naturally benefit from new construction in the area. Engineers are often part of the design process, for example, studying water runoff from new construction sites, conducting street design and traffic analyses, and a host of other development-related issues that come up. While there is always going to be business for engineers without a wave of new development, new development only means more business. Indeed, engineers tend to be growth oriented. They charge by the hour, and the more development going on, the more hours to charge. They will have a "pro-growth" bias.

Growth generates work for lawyers. Every developer needs to be represented by an attorney when meeting with the local municipality. Sometimes, the developer needs to appear in front of the Zoning Hearing Board when the development plan does not conform to all of the municipality's zoning laws. Such nonconformity can be as small as changing the size of parking spaces to problems such as water runoff due to overdevelopment of the property. Lawyers are usually employed by clients when property is bought or sold as well. Finally, more people mean more potential business for lawyers. Lawyers and engineers are part of the patronage system as they can be hired by municipalities, and as such, will be part of the growth-machine coalition.

The Local Media

Unless a newspaper has a national reputation like the *New York Times*, most newspapers are relatively fixed by the geographic area on which it reports. In order to increase the growth and stature of the local newspaper, circulation has to be increased within that relatively fixed geographic area. Moreover, advertising rates are tied to the size of a newspaper's circulation, so more development means more subscribers and more advertising. As such, the press has an *a priori* interest in growth and can be seen as a member of the coalition that comprises the growth machine.

Given the possibility of some subjectivity regarding news coverage of proposed development projects in local areas, newspapers can influence public opinion on the issue. During contested meetings over development projects or even demonstrations, what gets covered, who gets quoted, what pictures are shown, how those who oppose development are portrayed, are all areas where reporters and editors can influence readers. For example, when taking a picture of residents opposing a particular project, one can focus on someone who looks like the average citizen, or it can focus on a person who looks "freakish" with a spray-painted face or a controversial placard. Such a picture may be used to draw interest or increase circulation, but it would also influence perceptions of readers who could make subconscious decisions as to whether they see those who oppose the project as regular people like themselves or as people outside the mainstream. Editorials are other vehicles where newspapers can influence public opinion.

Trade Unions

Organized labor is also a member of the growth-machine coalition because of the jobs that such growth would provide. Particular support tends to come from the building trades, who especially benefit from development projects. In addition to jobs, the power and authority of local union leaders tend to grow, especially when a greater number of laborers will end up belonging to the local as a consequence of growth (Logan and Molotch, 1987: 81). Union leaders can be sometimes called upon by other members of the growth machine, particularly developers, to show support for development because of its ability to create jobs in general, and a specific development project in particular. This enlistment of support is particularly used when projects are under attack in specific local areas. Indeed, "job creation" becomes the mantra or ideology of the growth machine when projects are under attack, and the overarching value of job creation—not growth—becomes the issue (*Bucks County Courier Times,* May 26, 1983). While critics of this point consider this mantra for growth in the same vein as security of the country is used to defend every military expense, there is no question that creating and maintaining working-class jobs is an important goal, and jobs are indeed created by development projects (an overall assessment of this claim appears later). But one can also call into question the concern of developers for jobs, especially when it is primarily raised in times of contention, especially when efforts are made to use nonunion labor as well. Nevertheless, the creation and retention of jobs is the ideology of the growth machine, and job growth is used as the argument to convince the public to support growth-oriented projects. Organized labor, especially in the building trades, thus becomes part of the growth-machine coalition.

Local Museums, Hospitals and the Community College

Though educational institutions do not usually get overtly active in supporting growth, they do benefit from increased intensification of land use. Most community colleges only draw from the boundaries of the county in which they are located. Hence, more growth, more potential students, and the increased enrollment can be used to justify requests for additional faculty lines, more buildings and more administrative positions. Elected officials, who, as noted above, are members of the growth machine, appoint members of the Board of Directors for Community Colleges. These appointments are usually politically based appointments, so it is expected that those board members will not be opponents of growth, if not direct supporters of the process.

Local museums rely on the public for revenue whether in the form of admissions or by selling higher-level memberships (e.g., "Friends of the local museum"). The greater the growth in population, the greater potential there will be for support for the museum. While museum directors may not necessarily get directly involved in supporting growth, they would have to be cognizant of the benefits of growth for their institution.

Hospitals usually serve the local population. While not necessarily at the forefront of the growth machine, except through memberships to pro-growth organizations such as the Chamber of Commerce, hospitals clearly benefit from increased growth. Population growth not only means more potential customers, but also creates opportunities for the hospital to increase areas of specialization.

The growth coalition is not only a group interested in promoting land development, both residential and commercial, as well as favoring projects that expand the infrastructure of an area, but they also seek the support of local governments in legislating pro-development policies. Because governance in suburbs and small towns is largely controlled by "recognized elites," the political clout of the growth machine's interests is compatible with theirs as well (Mattson, 2002: 104). They tend to have access to large amounts of financial resources and they can use them for hiring top-notch lawyers and experts to argue their cause (Hawkins, 2014: 2505–2506). They "propagate an ideology of growth" as well as engage in tactical politics around local government land use, regulation to influence policy and decision making (Knox,

2008: 9). Creation of jobs is also part of their rationale when advocating for growth-related projects.

Members of the growth machine and their adherents can also lobby local officials on their own work time, while residents who oppose them have to use their available free time. The growth machine is a formidable force at the local level of government.

OPPOSITION TO THE GROWTH MACHINE

There is naturally opposition to the growth machine. Residents who fear that intensification of land use in their communities will threaten the intrinsic character of their communities, make up the chief opposition to the growth machine. This opposition tends to transcend differences among residents such as rank and file party affiliation, social class, religion and other variables that often tend to separate people in politics. Most residents in suburban areas thus support controlling growth in their areas (Baldassare, 1992: 485).

There are various threats that residents identify with growth. One concern involves the negative impact of growth on the overall environment. Such a concern can involve the loss of wildlife habitat or the increase in storm water runoff from proposed development into residents' homes. When wooded areas are cleared for housing or commercial development, residents also fear the loss of aesthetic value and concomitant property values (Duncan and Duncan, 2004: 85–93). In short, residents fear the overall character of their town can be undermined by the intensification of land use.

Research has confirmed that these fears associated with suburban growth and sprawl are warranted. Increased growth has led to a loss of open space and farmland, fewer amenities such as parks and public transit, traffic congestion, and higher taxes and water and sewer costs, among others (Burchell, et al., 2005: 102–113). Personal health is also impacted. Greater reliance on automobiles and less walking contribute to increasing obesity rates and concomitant health problems (Finkelstein and Zuckerman, 2008: 136–138). Traffic congestion can threaten public safety and many residents who move to the suburbs and still work in or near a city are subjected to a long inefficient commutes (White, 1978: 185).

Duaney et al. have declared that "developers somehow have devolved from admired figures into reviled characters, challenging drug dealers and pimps for position in the public's esteem" (2000: 100). The sprawl created by developers, with segregated areas of housing clusters, shopping centers, office parks, etc., forces residents to spend an unprecedented amount of time going from place to place (Duaney, et al., 2000: 5–7). Such single-use development is a product of single-use zoning that was sanctioned by a 1926 Supreme

Court case and later advocated by the Federal Housing Authority (Gallagher, 2014: 39–49). Putnam also identified suburban sprawl as a key component contributing to the loss of community in society (2000: 208–210).

Residents also oppose the growth machine because of the threats it presents to their "daily round" (Logan and Molotch, 1987: 20, 103–104). Shopping patterns, child care, schooling, and the general routes to go places are highly valued by residents and potential threats to this predictable array of services and goods available can lead to opposition to the intensification of land use. Neighborhood structure provides a sense of identity, and the threat to the overall character of a town also leads to opposition to the growth machine.

Residents may also fear the increased costs associated with increased development. Proponents of the growth machine point to the increase in "tax ratables" or more property owners paying taxes to the local area as a clear benefit to all residents. In other words, building more houses and commercial buildings leads to more property taxes being paid to the local government, and thereby contributing to the financial health of the area. There is some intuitive merit to this kind of reasoning. And in some isolated cases, this scenario is certainly the case. However, there are hidden, and often not so hidden, financial costs to increased development as well. First and foremost, increased development leads to the need to build new schools and hire additional teachers for them (Logan and Molotch, 1987: 86–88). Increased development only exacerbates the need to raise property taxes to support a growing school system. The need for increased police and fire protection, hospitals, the construction and maintenance of roads, sewers and other infrastructural also lead to need for increased taxes. Try to find anyone who says that their local, school and county taxes have not gone up over the years. Increased development only exacerbates these trends. Residents may oppose projects proposed by the growth machine because they fear the increased taxes that accompany such development.

Indeed, many of the claims made by proponents of the growth machine about the benefits of increased growth for the community as a whole tend to be unsubstantiated or outright false. For example, the promise of *sustained* job growth has not been substantiated (Logan and Molotch, 1987: 88–91). The numbers of jobs may initially go up during the construction phase, and they may even be sustained afterwards, but when the new population growth has been added, the overall employment rate remains the same. If the growth-related activity ends, the unemployment rate could even become higher than before. Intangible consequences such as added traffic congestion and widening of country roads may cause some areas to lose their local charm and uniqueness.

In addition to local residents, some small businesses tend to identify with the concerns of residents and support their opposition to growth. Their alliance with local residents can be linked to their day-to-day interaction with residents. These businesses may support opposition grassroots movements by donating supplies or taking out ads in newsletters. Small businesses may fear competition from larger box stores that located nearby as a consequence of increased population levels. These larger stores or chains can out-compete smaller businesses because they can buy in larger quantities causing their prices to be cheaper. For example, there was a time when there were many independently owned drug stores. Nowadays, drug stores are mainly large chains that have put the independent stores out of business. Wal-Mart, for example, has long been criticized for eliminating local businesses (e.g., Halebsky, 2004: 115–134). Large chains do not have the roots in the local community that privately owned independent stores have. They are less likely to support local causes and organizations such as the Little League, Boy and Girl Scouts and the local school's music programs as well.

Environmental groups have also become part of the opposition to the intensification of land use. Since the 1970s, preserving open space, farmland and wetlands has been seen by many groups as part of an overall environmental movement (Fishel, 2004: 332). It becomes a form of "acting locally" to a global environmental problem. Often, land trusts are developed to raise money to acquire open land and work with local governments to purchase undeveloped land with the intent of preserving it that way. They can also play an important role in advising local officials on environmental best practices and provide other related information (Hawkins, 2014: 2505).

Local governments recognize the need to address unchecked suburban sprawl, partly in response to residents and partly due to the lack of infrastructure in place with which to support such growth (Hawkins, 2014: 2503–2504). The concept of "smart growth" has been proposed to direct development projects away from these areas and reinvesting them in urban neighborhoods that have an infrastructure in place (Hawkins, 2014: 2504). Logan and Zhou also note that local governments regulate growth to preserve the level of community identity within their municipality (1989: 462). Such an approach would go against the interests of the growth machine. Humphrey has noted that the degree of opposition tends to correlate with social class, in that more affluent areas are able to put up a stronger resistance to the growth machine (2001: 99–121).

When you look at how the two sides are stacked up, it is difficult to see how residents can have a chance against the local growth machine. The growth machine has much more money and resources, and they have people employed full time to represent their interests at all stages of the process. The local opposition has less money and has to organize in their spare time, such as after work and on weekends. Local residents have to take time away from their normal routine such as spending time with their families, shopping and just plain relaxing.

Residents turn to their local government to defend their interests and thereby defend the character of their town. Indeed, it has been found that voters in these areas tend to be issue oriented (Oliver and Ha, 2007: 394). Even very conservative residents who oppose government interfering with the rights of private ownership when it comes to state and national politics often support the role of local government in protecting their interests against the growth machine. This "Not In My Back Yard" philosophical orientation runs deep in small towns, as residents may not be opposed to growth as a generic concept, but they are in their own locale (Baldassare, 1992: 485). Nonetheless, it does speak to the point that residents look to government for help with their struggle against the growth machine.

Opposition to the growth machine has also found its critics (e.g., Bruegman, 2005). Many of the same residents protesting further development in their community are living in that community because of previous development and intensified land use. In other words, critics contend that these protesters move into an area and then want to lock the door to development, locking out others from moving to the area. While pointing out that there is some level of protectionism in these efforts, critics also ignore the possibility that an area or community can become overdeveloped. Critics who argue that anti-development sentiment is simply protectionism serve as a useful *carte blanche* approach for developers. It also negates the possible merits of resident protest by attacking the motives of protesters instead of analyzing the substance of their concerns.

Critics have also raised other concerns about those who fight against development. While the conflict to preserve the character of one's community is real, which can make resistance to the growth machine a progressive movement, it can also be used as a means to maintain the status quo. Setting up rules against development can be seen as a way for residents to maintain social class and race/ethnic homogeneity in their communities. In other words, residents may be interested in excluding groups that they think will have adverse effects on their community. Hirt has found that race-based and class-based fears led to zoning laws as a way to prevent a lowering of property values (2014: 173). Duncan and Duncan, for example, suggest that protection of the "aesthetic" in a town may be a cover for maintaining exclusivity (2004: 88–90). Burchell et al found that residents pressure local government officials to adopt exclusionary zoning laws to protect the community from low-income housing (2005: 136).

Peck observes that racial and class exclusivity can be a product of both development and controls against it (2011: 903–905). Vicino also attributes exclusivity to development as well, including the development of "restrictive covenants" that are legal obligations incorporated into the deed of a house that stipulates rules sellers and buyers must abide by, and race discrimination can be one of those stipulations (Vicino, 2008: 371). White notes when new housing appears to be aimed at the construction of large single-family homes or luxury townhouses, the housing needs of the poor are ignored (1978: 186). Indeed socioeconomic housing segregation becomes heightened.

Modarres and Kirby question whether development of the post–World War II suburbs, including the objectives of both developers and local government officials, has facilitated the separation of American citizens by social class and race, or whether they merely reflect the polarization and segregation that have shaped American discourse for centuries (2009: 117).

There is merit to all these points of view. There is no question residents want to preserve their property values, and they rightly or wrongly identify maintaining exclusionary practices as a means to do so. On the other hand, developers and the growth machine seek to intensify land use as means to profit, and the consequences of development noted above can be collateral damage to their profit-making activities. Residents who fight such development are also defending their way of life.

The case studies of development projects in one small town presented below demonstrate different ways local government can get involved when there are development projects that are deemed against the overall well-being of the community. They are meant to illustrate ways in which local governments can prevent the growth machine from imposing its will on communities. As noted earlier, the main weapons available to local governments are the ordinances that govern development and the ability to hold projects up through the legal system. Bear in mind, these cases are not presented here to suggest that all development projects are opposed or seen as contrary to the needs of the town. Clearly, some development projects are supported.

While these cases may suggest that all development projects that intensify land use are seen as contrary to the interests of the town, most towns simply want to control or regulate development. Many plans get accepted, and there are times when companies and investors are encouraged to develop. When businesses deemed as likely to make a positive contribution to a town apply for a development permit, local governments can bend over backward to help. Some zoning codes, such as the amount of parking spaces needed for a business, can be waived or modified if officials want this plan to happen. However, there are also proposed development plans that residents and government officials see as potential threats to the residential character of the community. The weapons available to local government—enforcement of its zoning book, eminent domain laws, use of the courts and the time it provides, and grant money for the purchase of development rights or the land itself—while limited, can be and have been, useful to helping officials protect their visions for the community.

Zoning

Zoning has become a major way for municipalities to control or resist development. American values are such that issues of planning and zoning are the responsibility of local governments (Duncan and Duncan, 2004: 85–88). Local governments, through their planning commissions and elected officials establish a vision for their community and then pass a series of laws to realize this vision. The zoning book is a compilation of ordinances aimed at addressing the rules for development. They can encourage development with little constraints given to developers or they can be very restrictive. These zoning laws have to be reasonable and allow development activity, but it can be controlled and regulated development activity. For example, if elected officials in a municipality did not want cell phone towers, they would have to restrict them to certain areas, such as industrial districts. If they were banned outright, the zoning book could be tossed out in court for denying the constitutional rights of others, leaving a developer, or in this case, a cell phone company with *carte blanche* plans.

Development cannot be banned; the zoning book simply makes rules that can facilitate it or discourage it. Certain regulations can be spelled out, including a limitation of water runoff from the property to neighboring areas, establishment of a minimum size of parking spaces, the specification of the amount of land that a developer must provide as a buffer to adjacent properties, and the protection of wetlands and forests, among others. Some towns are clearly more protective of the environment than others, especially when residents are mobilized to elect environmentally friendly candidates. The conflict between the growth machine and residents and small businesses who oppose growth can become the basis for conflict in elections at the local level. However, conflict can also occur when development projects are submitted by developers as well and considered by government officials at public meetings.

While the construction of the zoning book is the principal way that local governments operationalize their vision for their community, local officials are also involved once plans are submitted. The Planning Commission may review the development plan to measure it against the vision of the town, as articulated in government plans as well as existing ordinances. Engineers and attorneys appointed by the local government are expected to review the plans very closely to ensure that local ordinances are followed. Although professionals like engineers and attorneys have been identified as part of the growth-machine coalition, locally elected officials have to make sure that the professionals they hire embody the values they hold. Local political conflicts over development can and do take place at every stage of the development process, from the approval of the overall plan, to the requests for building permits. Finally, elected officials render a decision based on all the input received from hearings and communications from professionals.

Case Study

In the early 1990s, a prominent non-profit school/residential home for patients with brain trauma that was located in the town faced financial shortfalls. In order to compensate for this shortfall, the school decided to sell some open space in town to a developer to build houses. Representatives for the school came to the Council with a plan to build a number of town homes on the property. The Borough Council was favorably disposed to the development plan, except for two aspects of their proposed plan. The first had to do with residents' complaints that part of the development would be built on what community members believed to be unmarked graves of Revolutionary War soldiers (General Washington brought troops to the town after the Battle of Trenton). The second problem was that the plan would take away too much property from an unused mansion that the school owned, and the fear was that the lack of land for parking would render the building unusable for subsequent buyers. Since the mansion was beginning to look in disrepair, the fear was that the building would continue to deteriorate. No investor was likely to find a suitable use for the property, other than a primary residence, and the overall costs of renovating and keeping up a house of this magnitude would be a detriment.

At the public hearing for the development plan, residents came out in force to protect what they believed to be the burial grounds for the revolutionary soldiers. Petitions signed by numerous residents accompanied the spoken concerns raised by those attending the meeting. Their position was partly based on a diary written by a resident in the late 1800s that described events that had taken place as observed from the view of a window across the street from her home as told by her grandfather. While there was some credibility to the diary, those who wanted to develop the property were not going to be stopped on the basis of a teenager's diary from the early 1800s. They took a photocopy of the diary and at the next meeting declared that their calculations had determined that the parking lot for a store on the street was already built over these unmarked mass graves. The Council voted by a narrow 4–3 margin to defend the claims of the residents and preserve that area of open space as the resting home for the Revolutionary War soldiers. To break the impasse, an agreement was made to hire an archeologist from a nearby university to check the area for possible mass graves. The archeologist had 7 days to make a recommendation, and both sides agreed to honor the findings. If there were mass graves, then the area would be donated to the town and preserved as a cemetery for the soldiers. If there was no evidence of graves, then that area of land could be part of the development plan. On the final day of the dig, evidence of mass graves was unearthed and the property was donated to the town as a Revolutionary War Cemetery.

The other concern did not lead to an amicable solution. Members of council strongly argued that taking away what could be used as parking area for the mansion would prevent a long-term viable use for the building. If the lot (two town houses) close to the mansion was to be stricken from the development plan, the remainder of the plan would get approval. The non-profit organization's attorney rejected the compromise and kept the development plan (without the area that would be the historic cemetery). The Council thereby rejected the plan, which prompted an immediate court appeal by the applicant. In court, the town's attorney argued that the proposed plan would limit the possible use of the mansion to a private one family residence, which is allowed in the Zoning Book. Government officials argued this option would be unsuitable given the building's size and the amount of renovations needed. The town saw viability for the building as a set of offices, a bed and breakfast or other uses that would require sufficient off-street parking that would be eliminated by the development plan. The organization's attorney argued that it is within the constitutional rights of the organization to try to have that building marketed as a private residence. The Borough brought up another variance that were violated; a cluster of trees to be cut down for the planned development violated a forest ordinance that limited number of trees planned to be cut down within a quarter acre lot. As discussed earlier, judges in the state tend to be pro-development and the judge in this case ruled in favor of the school's development plans. The town decided to appeal the lower court's decision to a higher court, with only a long shot hope of having the initial ruling overturned. While the chances of getting the ruling overturned were slim, the decision to go ahead with the appeal held up the project. By tying it up, the hope was that there would be further negotiations to help keep the lot of the mansion bigger so that it could accommodate more possible usages. Those negotiations never really took place, and while the town lost again in its appeal, the school's financial picture improved over this period and the entire development project was abandoned, thereby saving the open space. The Revolutionary War Cemetery was still donated to the town and, while the lot size of the mansion remained as drawn in the plans, its ownership changed hands a few times. With a further zoning change the property ultimately became a restaurant in town. Despite the lengthy legal process, the town and the school nonetheless still enjoy a good working relationship.

Eminent Domain

Another option available to local government to check or control development projects is the right to condemn properties by declaring "eminent domain." This tactic allows local governments to acquire property without the owner's consent if the government can argue the property would be used for the overall public good. Often times, governments exercise this right to build highways, schools, airports and ball parks. As this strategy became more popular in the 1990s, many state governments have adopted measures that limit the ability of local governments to use eminent domain (Lameiros, 2007: 8–10). However, it can also be exercised to preserve open space, create parks and thereby maintain the overall character of the town. This option prevents development, but it requires the municipality to get the property appraised and to pay fair market value to the property owner/developer. There is naturally some risk with using this option as one does not know the purchase price until the market value has been determined, and then that amount must be paid. Many small towns simply cannot afford to exercise this option. Most towns are not sitting on heaps of cash. Sometimes, a local government can work closely with a grassroots environmental group that is dedicated to purchasing open space to accomplish this option.

Case Study

A developer purchased a six acre lot that was ensconced within a block of the town that was a little over one square mile. Most of the houses in town were located on the perimeter of the block and the lot, though privately owned, had remained vacant since the 1700s. It was marked by running streams, wetlands and wildlife within it. For years, children (and adults) played within the area, damming up the stream with rocks, or hiking and playing on the property. The developer bought the lot from the company that had owned the land and proposed a development plan that included approximately 30 town homes on the property. Such development would violate many ordinances, including the destruction of wetlands, creation of too much water runoff onto neighboring properties, and several ordinances regarding buffers and side yards to neighboring properties, among others. The development plan that was submitted was virtually ripped apart by the Planning Commission, Engineer, and local residents and organizations. While some members of council were motivated by a desire to preserve the land as open space, others merely wanted to follow the ordinances of the town.

Hearings over the development plan were very contentious. Unlike most hearings, basic components of the plan, such as the calculations by the developer's engineers were challenged. Indeed, changes to the plan were made during the course of the hearings. This contentious atmosphere made potential compromise unlikely. The developer wanted to move ahead using his plan. The council unanimously denied the application on the basis that the plan violated many of the town's ordinances. The developer appealed the decision, and during the hearing, the judge told the attorneys for both parties to try and work out a compromise. Attempts were then made to compromise.

The developer offered to reduce the number of town houses to be built, but the town's engineer continued to find serious problems with the revised plan. Moreover, the developer did not really seem to seriously consider any ideas being suggested by council members. There was clearly an impasse and it looked pretty certain that the case was going back to court.

While the town's solicitor was confident of her ability to demonstrate in court the failure of the development plan to conform to the zoning ordinances, the judge's decision still presented a risk. Despite the obvious flaws of the plan, there was always a fear that a judge sympathetic to developers might simply deny the appeal, and arbitrarily pick a number of houses that could be built. In other words, the judge, who may not have had any experience in examining building plans, would make the compromise that had been earlier requested by the developer. On the other hand, the developer ran the risk that the court would rule in favor of the town, which would send him back to the drawing board and further prolong the amount of time when money used to acquire the property would be tied up.

In an effort to avoid these possibilities, discussions ensued to determine if the town could purchase the land. Both the town and the developer chose appraisers to determine the market value of the property. The appraisals came in within $50,000 of each other, very close considering that the value was appraised slightly below $1,000,000. A local non-profit organization committed to preserving open space immediately applied for grants at the local and state levels in order to raise the money necessary to buy the property. The developer, however, argued that both appraisers underestimated the worth of the property and demanded more than what the appraisers deemed as the worth of the property. In order to avoid the proverbial "rolling of the dice" in court, the council took a "wait and see" approach in order to know whether awarded funds would produce sufficient money to meet his demands. They neither accepted nor rejected the offer. Underlying use of this strategy was a belief that the housing market was likely to weaken considerably over this time, and the developer might accept a lower amount because of the growing risk associated with a weaker market. Again, time was on the side of the town's government. Within nine months, the local organization received grants from both the county and the state, and then chose to contribute additional money acquired through fundraising. They offered an amount that was only slightly above the appraised figures. Given the uncertainty of the market at the time as well as the shared risk of appealing the decision the possibility that Council might reject the project, the developer accepted the lower figure. In the end, a compromise occurred, and the local non-profit organization purchased the property on behalf of the town. The developer made a profit on land that was purchased but never developed, and the town preserved open space without using local tax payer money.

One should note that the success of a town having a nonprofit organization that can work effectively with local, county and state governments to secure grants is due in large part to having experienced, talented people in town as well as a population that can make financial contributions to support such an effort. More affluent communities are thus more likely to be able to preserve the character of their towns when confronting the growth machine. Lesser affluent towns may have fewer weapons at their disposal.

Delay Tactics

Another option available to local government is to turn down a developer's application, which forces the developer to go to court to appeal the decision. Officials cannot simply turn down a developer's plan because they do not like it. The plan must be in violation of the town's ordinances. Otherwise, the developer can sue elected officials as individuals for denying his/her constitutional rights. Normally, elected officials are indemnified from their decisions, and it is the town that gets sued, not the people involved. However, when there are no legal grounds for these decisions, the individuals themselves are indeed personally liable.

If the application is formally denied by the local town, the developer can appeal that decision. This process can be very time-consuming. It can take over a year before the case is heard and then several additional months before a decision is rendered. If the town's decision is overturned, the local government can appeal that court's decision to a higher court, holding the development up even more. The whole process can take five years or more before the matter is fully resolved. That is a long time for a developer to have an investment tied up, and it can be very frustrating to sit and wait. Developers like to buy a property, build something, make a profit and move on to the next property. Holding a development project up in court delays this process up and may indeed be the most effective weapon local government has.

Developers may be willing to compromise in order to get the project going. This predicament for developers gives government officials time to limit and shape the development in ways that may be more acceptable to local residents. In addition, the business and real estate climate for housing and office buildings can change. Of course, a town's decision to hold the process up by going to court is never done solely for purposes of delaying a process. It is only to defend the integrity of the town's ordinances (wink wink). Sometimes a "community benefit agreement" or "CBA" is negotiated between a developer and local government officials and/or local groups who might initially oppose the project. The developer might agree to make some form of environmental or other improvement in the town in exchange for either support or a promise not to oppose the development plan (Been, 2010: 5–6). This type of agreement has also been criticized as constituting a "zoning for sale" trend that lacks transparency (Been, 2010: 31).

When small towns go to court with developers the overall laws that define the rules by which development can take place are pro-development. In addition, judges who get to render judgments on these cases tend to be pro-development as well. State law supercedes local law when it comes to development, and state law will almost always "water down" what the town requires. For example, the way wetlands are defined can vary. A small town takes a very comprehensive approach for an area to be considered a wetland. If a parcel of land has sitting water on the premises or has vegetation that is typically adapted for life in wetland environments, then a town can define that land as wetland. There are a number of restrictions for developers when wetlands are involved; they are protected. At the state level, however, the federal guidelines for wetlands are used. The federal guidelines consider areas to be wetlands only if the Army Corps of Engineers has surveyed the area and considered the water to be part of the waters of the United States. The Army Corps only considers waters that are large in scope and run into federal floodplains. A little tiny wetland within a small town is much less likely to have ever been seen by the Army Corps and therefore it never gets into their registry. As a consequence, a developer can successfully argue in court that the town's regulations regarding wetlands do not apply to the proposed development because, according to state law, there are no wetlands on the property. The statewide Municipal Planning Code (MPC), which is the statewide planning rule book, supercedes local ordinances. The MPC does not even address wetlands, only water courses and floodplains. There are the key environmental differences in this distinction: small towns would want to protect the property adjacent to the stream, and the wetlands vegetation growing on it, and not merely the stream itself.

Another less obvious example where courts and judges can exercise pro-development powers concerns trees and forests. Many towns can enact ordinances that are aimed at protecting the few trees and forests remaining within their borders. The MPC, however, requires each town to allow forestry as a matter of right for property owners in all zoning districts, thereby undermining the very intent of local municipalities to protect natural resources. While state laws may be stronger in local areas that are relatively undeveloped and have few guidelines that control development, areas that have experienced development and have tried to control increasing intensification of land use will tend to have stronger laws. And the state laws do not help towns take on the growth machine.

Judges who hear these appeals may not be well versed in zoning law issues. Their backgrounds could be in criminal law. As such, they may not fully understand zoning issues and might force a compromise between two parties rather than sit down and understand the complicated issues involved. They also may fall back on weaker state laws when rendering a verdict as well.

In some states, such as in Pennsylvania, judges run for office and need campaign donations to run a successful campaign. Members of the growth machine may happen to be big contributors to these campaigns, and the filtering process of identifying appropriate candidates associated with running for office suggests that judges who get elected may be sympathetic to the interests of developers. Indeed, even state legislators receive such contributions and that could very well explain why state laws tend to be more pro-development than those of local municipalities. Indeed, especially in small towns where state representatives and judges tend to come from the same party, although both major parties can be part of the growth-machine coalition.

Some local elected officials and influential citizens in local towns may appear to take a pro-environment, anti-growth machine view at the local level, but their party loyalty compels them to lend support for their party's candidates for state office and judgeships. These latter candidates tend to undermine their efforts to control development at the local level. This support can take subtle and not so subtle forms, for example, walking around town with candidates, putting up lawn sides in front of their homes or working the polls on Election Day to encourage neighbors to vote for these candidates. This party loyalty insures their popularity with these candidates and with party officials as a whole, but when these local candidates get elected and re-elected, they often toe the "party line" at the state level. That party line is very likely to be pro-development. In other words, some of these local officials may "talk the talk" at the local level and support the zoning laws that protect the town from over intensification of land use, but they also support candidates for higher offices who then may tend to water down state laws that undercut their own local interests.

CONCLUSION

The nature of political conflict may differ at the local level from the national level. The growth machine is made up of a coalition of businesses and building-trade-oriented labor interests. Residents and other businesses try to curtail or control their efforts. Forces advocating growth clearly have more resources at their disposal, but when organized, residents have the numbers to elect government officials to represent their interests.

Local governments can enact various zoning laws to help control the efforts of the growth machine to intensify land use in local communities. The case studies illustrated the ways in which local governments can help prevent the growth machine from imposing its will on communities. These cases may suggest that all development projects that intensify land use are seen as contrary to the interests of the town, but that scenario is not the case. Many indeed, get accepted, and there are times that companies and investors are encouraged to develop. When businesses deemed a positive contribution to a town applies for a development permit, some zoning codes such as the amount of parking spaces needed, etc. get waived because they are seen as beneficial to the town. However, there are proposed development plans that residents and government officials see as potential threats to the residential character of the community. The weapons of the local government to enforce its zoning book, to use time, and to seek grant money for the purchase of development rights or the land itself, while limited, can be and have been useful to helping officials protect their visions for the community. However, these same efforts can also maintain social class exclusivity in these communities.

Chapter 3

Making a Difference

Progressive Politics

Some aspects of the work of elected officials at the level of local government transcend politics. For example, there is no Democratic way to have garbage collected as opposed to a Republican way. There was just the right way to do it (though the degree to which recycling is a priority among elected officials can vary). A key essential job of local government is to provide and maintain basic services for its residents, and the technical problems that may be associated with these tasks transcend differences in political ideology.

Much of local government work is centered on the delivery of basic services, such as garbage collection, police protection, street sweeping and paving, and park and open space maintenance. Government officials also play a role in monitoring new construction as well as the remodeling of existing homes to ensure that safety standards are met. Emergency preparations are also important. For example, during snowstorms, streets must be plowed effectively as well. The political affiliation of local officials would probably have little impact on how to devise a plan to organize these functions effectively. Ideological differences between elected officials would be set aside.

While there are many government functions that local officials—regardless of party affiliation—might run the same way, there are, however, areas where the values and political philosophies of elected officials can make a difference not only in the way government is run, but also how residents of that town are affected.

As noted in the previous chapter, one key difference among local government officials is in the way they view development and the efforts of the growth machine to intensify land use in the town. Some local politicians are steadfastly suspicious of anything proposed by the growth machine. They fear the consequences of development on the character of the town. Others have other equally sincere convictions and favor development as a way to broaden the tax base of the community or they simply see positive benefits from growth itself. Of course, the degree of development that already exists within the town must always be considered as well.

Thus, there are important differences among local officials, and the nature of the town is going to be affected differently depending upon who is running the show. This difference is not due to differences in competence (though obviously there are differences in capabilities), but rather to differences in approaches based on values and political philosophies that local officials bring to governing a town.

Moreover, some local officials are hesitant to work for change, much less to be change catalysts. They are content with maintaining the status quo. It is certainly easier to keep doing things (and not doing things) the way they have been done in the past, as the learning curve for governing a town is a lot lower. Change requires venturing into less chartered waters. Nonetheless, one might run for local office with the intention of changing things. After winning an election, the electoral victory is then seen as a mandate to implement those desired changes. However, the road to change is not necessarily a smooth one.

Getting elected to local government also does not provide a context where change happens easily. And the smaller the level of government, the less likely elected officials are to be able to make significant social change. A small town is affected too much by the larger social and economic forces in society as well as by the actions of county, state and federal governments. Moreover, revenues mainly come from taxes, and the duties of local government include providing for the safety of its residents, regulating development, issuing building permits, maintaining the streets and collecting trash. Elected officials must work within this overall context and cannot always expect to change things easily. Moreover, other elected officials may have different agendas and interests, which could dampen or resist the pace of change. Immediate needs, such as a budget crisis, can also redirect one's priorities or place budgetary restraints on changes that can be implemented.

Nevertheless, elected officials can have a very positive impact by putting "politics in command" at the local level. In other words, one's values and political commitment can at times make a difference and be a positive force in helping to solve problems. And if a number of elected officials work for positive changes in many local municipalities, their efforts can add up to become a positive source of real social change in some ways. The more local one acts, the fewer the overbearing issues to overcome, as opposition can be fragmented due to the configuration of groups in that locality. For example, there may not be a critical mass of residents willing to take on elected officials.

Individuals previously involved in grassroots movements in the past may seek elected office as a means to extend the goals of that movement by using the powers of local government to help implement desired changes. Local grassroots movements face ongoing obstacles that can impede their success. Those engaged in these movements usually have job and family responsibilities and their activism constitutes an extracurricular activity. Eventually, people burn out or have to reduce the extent of their commitment to focus on their other responsibilities that may have been neglected. Grassroots movements also rely on voluntary financial contributions from residents and other members to keep the movements' activities afloat. Passion versus resources: there are strengths and limitations when grassroots movements tried to implement change (see, for example, Feola and Nunes, 2014: 232–250). Running for election and using the local government as a vehicle for implementing goals can be effective as these offices are staffed with employees. There is access to professionals, such as attorneys and engineers.

Activists can still be effective in influencing local governments. By lobbying, attending government meetings, circulating petitions, etc., activists who are not elected officials can apply considerable pressure on local government officials to support changes. Moreover, those in local government can increasingly invest in the local population by strategically and effectively enabling increased civic engagement (Sirianni, 2009: 2–10). While government officials can get elected and put "politics in command" they can create the opportunities to encourage the engagement of their citizens to be active as well. Sirianni provides a number of reasons why governments at all levels need to become more effective enablers of civic engagement. The trends toward traditional forms of civic engagement (e.g., involvement in community associations, volunteer groups, local political campaigning) have been negative (Putnam, 2000). Because increased civic engagement will not necessarily "bubble up from the wellsprings of civil society," government involvement can act as a catalyst to engage citizens (Sirianni, 2009: 37). Empowerment of citizens by local governments also goes a long way to overcoming the belief that governments set up barriers to involvement, and they can help overcome the problems faced by citizen groups who do not have enough resources (Sirianni, 2009: 8–13).

There have been an increasing number of activists running for elected office and becoming directly part of government decision making. Flacks observes that beginning in the 1970s, activists began running for local office as a means to directly influence government decision making, particularly in university or college towns (Flacks, 1995: 254–5). Activists made alliances with other progressive social movements in the 1980s for similar effects in other types of cities. Accounts of how progressive groups affect meaningful changes in cities such as Santa Cruz, California (Gendron and Domhoff, 2009), Hartford (CT), Burlington (VT) and Berkeley (CA), (Clavel, 1986) have been documented. The accounts tend to focus on medium-sized cities that are large enough to offer a vast array of social services and small enough that activists can mount a successful campaign. Little systematic work has examined how those running for elected office in small towns can impact the direction of smaller sized municipalities. Small towns may not offer the array of services, such as public housing, social services or a large job sector, but there are still areas where an impact can be made.

This chapter examines the progressive initiatives introduced in small cities, suburban areas and small towns in Langhorne and how putting "politics in command" can make a difference at the local level of government. Key areas for change that will be addressed include the environment and housing, among others.

ENVIRONMENT

One key area where local municipalities can have an important impact is the environment. There are a number of ways that one can use local governments to be a positive force in protecting the environment, including the type of energy purchased for the municipality, conservation practices and legislation protecting the environment, among others. Indeed, the bumper stick "Think Globally, Act Locally" encourages people to respond to such important issues where they can. Working to protect the environment is so important because the damage to it can be irreversible. While there are other important issues, such as health care and jobs, none have the longer lasting implications than the destruction of the environment.

There are natural limitations faced by local governments when they try to introduce measures that address the environment. There is no question that the problems associated with the environment must be attributed to economic and political forces that go well beyond the purview of local governments. Environmental problems, such as water and air pollution as well as climate change, are too geographically dispersed. Without concerted action by most local governments, changes made at the local level can have very limited impact. Laws and regulations that are passed can only be enforced within the boundaries of that local area. Moreover, state laws can explicitly preclude local governments from taking some kinds of environmental actions, particularly if they are inconsistent with those established at the state level (Flatt, 2008: 458). While there often can be congruence between the policies at the state level and most local governments, those local governments that may intend to take a leadership role in addressing the environment would be preempted by state law from doing so.

Despite the limitations of local government of being part of the long-term solution to problems associated with climate change, there is an important role that local governments can and have played. During the 1980s, for example, the Environmental Justice Movement targeted local threats to the environment. The focus of the movement was on local government (Mihaylov and Perkins, 2015: 124). The problems, whether unhealthy water or air, or other forms of pollution, are affected locally and the major recourse that activists have is on the local level. Mihaylov and Perkins observe "local communities therefore are important agents and contexts of environmental politics" (2015: 127) and much of their attention includes citizens and activist groups putting pressure on local government. Flatt notes that local government officials are more likely to have personal contact with companies that can have adverse effects on the environment and can thereby be more effective in advancing positive measures regarding the environment (Flatt, 2008: 456).

The limitations of local governments in enacting progressive measures regarding the environment, as noted above, can also become a strength. While larger political entities, such as the national, state and even county levels can be much more heterogeneous in terms of political diversity, local governments may have abilities to enact progressive change because of their smallness. Local government officials may have larger percentages of citizens in favor of environmental action and thus have fewer political obstacles to overcome. They are closer to their citizens than those in state and federal government and more distant from lobbyists that might oppose environmental regulation, such as those in industries that rely on fossil fuels (Saha, 2009: 20). Threats to the environment are also felt locally. Many environmental projects have often been initiated by local citizens and organizations that see working on a local level is a way to address larger dominant economic and political forces (Portney, 2005: 584). Moreover, local governments may have fewer bureaucratic obstacles to overcome because of the smaller scope of government.

Because of their closeness to citizens and local activist groups, many local governments have made a priority of incorporating "sustainability" into their government practices. Indeed, sustainability has become a goal endorsed by many environmental groups and religious organizations (Klein, 2014: 47,55; Edwards, 2005: 29–47; Pope Francis, 2015: 85–100). The World Commission on Environment and Development defines sustainable development as "development that meets the needs of the present without compromising the ability of future generations to meet their own needs" (quoted in Saha, 2009: 18). A United Nations resolution also sees the connection between the local government and the environment: "Local authorities construct, operate and maintain economic, social, and environmental infrastructure, oversee planning processes, establish local environmental policies and regulations, and assist in implementing national and subnational environmental policies" (cited in Portnoy, 2005: 581). Such a priority shapes land-use development, policies toward polluters of the environment as well as taking a more holistic approach to all aspects of government, such as in social equity concerns, intergovernmental coordination and fostering a sense of community. Such an overarching approach affects everything from trash collection and recycling to new construction of housing and office buildings.

Local governments from big cities to small towns have taken a number of initiatives to have a positive effect on the environment. Many municipalities, for example, have committed to constructing new buildings using the Leadership in Energy and Environmental Design (LEED) certification system that has been developed by the U.S. Green Building Council in Washington, D.C. (Stansberry, 2005: 40–46). The criteria can be met by using cool or green roofs, energy management and cogeneration, and using a community-owned electric utility, among others. Austin Texas, for example, requires all municipal buildings to meet LEED criteria (http://austintexas.gov/page/green-capital-improvement-projects).

An international organization, ICLEI Local Governments for Sustainability is a membership association made up of counties and large and small cities and towns that have made a commitment to sustainable development (www.iclei.org). As an encompassing association, ICLEI provides networking, programs and the tools to help local governments meet their goals of sustainability. The number of local governments, representing large cities and small towns, that have engaged in activities aimed at preserving the environment is so large, a listing of these local governments would be nearly impossible. One could note the accomplishments, however, by acknowledging the recognition given by leading organizations.

ICMA (International City/County Management Association) located in Washington, D.C. recognizes local governments that engage in environmental practices that meet the needs of the present without compromising future generations (see ICMA.org). Because the ability of local governments to enact pro-government initiatives is affected by the size of the population and subsequent resources available, awards are given by population size. For example, a city such as Davenport, Iowa can be recognized for adding hybrid cars to their pool cars and recycling recovered methane. For populations less than 10,000 residents, High Springs, Florida was recognized for its commitment to creating a local farmer's market for residents to purchase locally grown produce and for the creation of community gardens.

American City and County is an online publication with municipalities as its intended audience that reports on environmental initiatives that local governments have undertaken. It becomes evident that there are countless ways that local governments can introduce measures that can have a positive impact on the environment. These include the transformation of landfills into solar farms in Maryland (*American City and* County, August, 2015), the development of a residential food scrap collection service for composting in Hoboken, NJ (May, 2015) and the installation of solar panels on municipal buildings in Park City, Utah (May, 2015). Numerous cities and towns have recognized the virtue of building new parks as a form of conservation and community development (June, 2015). Other municipalities have invested in bike share stations to reduce reliance on automobile use (June, 2015), reducing paper use by becoming "fiber towns" (July, 2015), recycling battery programs (May, 2015) are additional ways that local governments can get involved. The possibilities are endless.

There are many nonprofit organizations that give awards to local governments to recognize their commitment to the environment as well as to encourage others to follow their lead. In the Commonwealth of Pennsylvania, Citizens for Penn's Future (PENNfuture) was formed in 1998 to help create a just future that integrates the economy, the environment and communities. The organization also recognizes local businesses that engage in practices that demonstrate commitment to the environment. In addition to their advocacy of various social policies, the organization also acknowledges the contributions that local governments have made to protect and sustain the environment. Municipalities have been recognized for purchasing renewable forms of energy.

Case Study

One immediate way that local governments can positively impact the environment is the way in which they purchase municipal energy. The town became the first municipality east of California to purchase electricity from 100 percent renewable forms of energy, such as solar or wind. A state level pro-environment nonprofit organization, Penn Future, awarded the town "Best Government Entity" for the example it set for all other forms of government. The town received great press, and members of council and the mayor enjoyed the accolades given at a fancy luncheon where the award was given. Nonetheless, the road to this decision was not necessarily without its bumps.

When the issue was first brought up at a council meeting, its reception was mixed. The vote to move to 100 percent renewable forms of energy ended with a 3–3 tie (one member of council was absent) and the mayor, who gets to break tie votes, decided to vote against the measure. There were a number of reasons offered by opponents. First, there was concern about stepping on the toes of the local utility company, who would lose business. Personnel from the company occasionally did favors for local officials, such as trimming trees on the main streets that were near power lines. Some officials who interact with local utility officials would no doubt feel embarrassed about switching to another company, and whatever political ties that were there would be weakened. In other words, the personal ties connected with the "old buddy system" would be threatened by the pro-environment initiative. The "old buddy system" definitely exists, and as such, it serves as a force for the preservation of the status quo. The more politically entrenched local officials are, the more of a force this system is in decision-making. Cronyism as a social force in local politics is an impediment to social change.

A second concern cited by council members was the possible increase in costs. In 2001, the cost for 100 percent renewable electricity was actually higher than the cost for electricity that came from nuclear and/or coal power plants. Intuitively, one would expect renewable energy to be cheaper, but the cost per kilowatt hour for the "greener" energy was slightly more. The economies of scale for renewable energy technology have not yet been reached yet. By switching to "greener" energy, local governments could help encourage increased capital investment in renewable energy in the market place, which would reduce energy expenses in the long run. However, at the time, the municipal electric bill would be higher for "going green."

All of these arguments were made when the motion to switch to green energy was brought up the first time around. "Old time politics" was the winner by virtue of the tie and the mayor, (who breaks tie votes) supporting the status quo. However, two months later, a local high school senior (my daughter!) came to a council meeting with a science teacher from the high school. This young citizen made a passionate case arguing that council members who voted to stay with the current arrangement regarding municipal energy were leaving the environmental damage to her generation. The high school teacher backed up her argument with technical information.

Two key differences occurred between the time of the initial discussion when the attempt to switch providers failed, and the second, when it succeeded. First, all seven members of council were in attendance at the second vote, and the one who missed the previous meeting supported the switch to 100 percent renewable energy. The second difference was that the presence of the press at the second meeting. When the issue was brought up the first time, it was late in the evening, and local reporters covering the council meeting had gone home. At the second meeting, the issue came up early and reporters were in full attendance. All votes and quotes would be seen in the next day's papers. It is one thing to be for old time cronyism at the expense of the environment when no one is around to hear or quote it; it is another when your position will be presented in the newspaper, where one can forever bring it to your attention. Needless to say, there was a new motion to switch the municipality's energy to a provider that supplied 100 percent renewable energy, and this time the vote was unanimous! When the council and mayor were invited to a fancy luncheon to receive our wonderful award, those in other towns were encouraged to go to their government meetings and request that their elected officials also switch to 100 percent renewable energy.

Privately, we told them that bringing children to help make the case would not hurt their effort, and to make sure the press was there!

There are other ways to "act locally" and make a positive impact on the environment. How garbage, or what is called solid waste by insiders, is collected can also make a difference. Decision to encourage recycling of glass, plastics and newspapers by negotiating contracts with the municipal trash hauler to bring a separate truck into the town just for recyclables is one strategy. Containers can be distributed to all homes free of charge so they had a bin for the recyclables. While the degree to which recycling contributes to the environment can be debated, having the municipality encourage it in these ways is certainly a positive effort (e.g., Ross and Evans, 2003; Tonglet, Philips and Bates, 2004). Recycling does reduce the amount of overall refuse for the municipality that is sent to the landfill, and since recyclables can be later resold by the trash hauler, the costs of trash pickup can potentially be less than having the same materials getting sent to the landfill.

The same argument can be made for yard waste. Many towns allow burning of yard waste, such as brush and leaves (at one time residents of small towns and rural areas also burned trash). Banning the burning of yard waste makes common sense. Not only does it make a small contribution to limiting emission of carbon dioxide into the air, neighbors—especially those with respiratory problems—are adversely affected by the burning. However, when local governments prevent residents from burning leaves, fallen limbs and other brush, residents then have to be provided with a legal outlet for getting rid of them. The solid waste contract with the trash hauler can include the pick up of grass, leaves, small limbs and other such yard waste. A clause in the contract can also require that yard waste that was collected has to be taken somewhere where it would be left to breakdown naturally and not be burned elsewhere. Some towns simply pick up yard waste, especially leaves, by having residents rake them to the curb for easy pick up as an alternative way to deal with this matter. Residents could no longer claim that yard waste had to be burned with either of these local government initiatives. Moreover, under these types of initiatives, residents have a viable alternative to burning waste, and its banning should not face too much resistance from residents. While weekly recycling of yard waste does add a small charge to the cost of trash pickup, the increase is negligible and serves as a small way to help the environment. The issue of Freon in refrigerators and air conditioners can also be addressed in a similar way.

OPEN SPACE

Protecting open space and wetlands is an additional goal that local communities can pursue in various ways (Tarlock, 1993). Elected officials can use ordinances that can protect the environment in a number of ways. Towns are allowed to designate certain areas as open space, providing those areas were open prior to that designation. Anyone wanting to convert open space to houses or a shopping center must then get the town to approve the rezoning to a different use. A developer can also go to the town's Zoning Hearing Board for a variance. The Zoning Board is made up of local residents, and will often be under pressure to but not go against the wishes of an irate group of residents who oppose the plan. The smaller the municipal area, the more likely board members will know residents at the meeting personally, adding to the pressure.

Another way to protect the environment is by demanding less or no additional water runoff in a development plan. Open space is a pervious structure where water can seep (engineers call this "percolate") into the ground. Development creates impervious structures that could cause water runoff and sometimes flooding in neighboring properties. By demanding that there be no more, or even less water runoff after any development, the local environment is protected. A developer would have to submit a water runoff plan provided by one's own engineer that demonstrates the water runoff requirements are met. The town's engineer, whose time is also paid for by the developer, would have to approve that plan. The evaluation by the town's engineer is not affected because the developer is paying for the engineer's time, because payment is often made through an escrow payment at the time of application to develop the property. The existence of escrow funds prevents towns from going broke evaluating developer's plans, and threatening towns to compromise their evaluation of the plans as a cost-saving strategy. In other words, if a town had to constantly pay for its engineer to evaluate a developer's plans, and the town did not have a large reservoir of money to support such activity, a town might be pressured financially to merely accept the work of the developer's engineer as sufficient. Yet a developer's engineer is paid by the developer and can hardly be expected to write a report indicating that the plans are not in compliance with the water runoff ordinances of the town. Hence, the town needs its own engineer to make an independent assessment of the plan, even with a critical eye toward the developer's proposal. An effective council should know that the engineer's report is the first line of defense, and the engineer should be reminded that all the town's ordinances should be strictly enforced. Note the discussion of an application to build thirty townhomes on open space in the previous chapter.

Another way zoning ordinances can help protect the environment is by the way various environmental terms are defined and interpreted. For example, as noted in chapter 2, "wetlands" can defined in various ways (see Toliver, 1993). It can simply mean that there has to be sitting water on the property. It can also be used to designate areas where wildlife consistent with that of wetlands is on the property. The latter definition protects the town from occasional droughts where sitting water might temporarily dry out. While the state government, which might be more likely to be influenced by the interests of developers, may take a more limited and restrictive definition, such as the one that requiring sitting water to be the criterion establishing a wetland, the local government can take a stronger stance by accepting the more inclusive definition of wetlands. That definition may be challenged by developers in court, but it at least gives the community a fighting chance to protect its environment.

Many ideas regarding zoning come from recommendations made by other commissions in town. For example, as noted previously, the town's Planning Commission meets specifically to address the long-range needs of the town (which includes the desire to protect the environment as well as the historic character of the town). The commission can explore planning issues in much greater depth than what can take place in council meetings, and its members may be appointed because of particular expertise in these matters. The Planning Commission can take a proactive view that can anticipate the changes proposed by developers that may take place in time, and be prepared for those changes, rather than simply reacting to changes that are immediately taking place. A Planning Commission may prepare for a major development project that may be proposed in town long before such a project is actually submitted. Attention can be given to determine whether current ordinances still protect the interests of the residents. For example, a zoning book written in the 1970s could not have anticipated the growth in the installment of cellular towers in communities. As such, there would be no regulation of cell towers because they are not mentioned in the zoning ordinances. A proactive Planning Commission might recommend new rules regarding their placement that would protect the town prior to a company proposing to put one in town.

Cellular towers are still controversial because there is still no consensus regarding the long-term health consequences of exposure to them (Wolf and Wolf, 2004; Levitt and Lai, 2010). While a knee-jerk reaction might be to ban cellular towers from the town altogether, such a ban would violate the constitutional rights of cell phone companies who need to place towers in certain areas in order to provide consistent service to their customers. Indeed, while local government officials may oppose their presence in their town, they probably also have a cell phone in their pocket and prefer non-interrupted service. The key for a local government is to work with the Planning Commission in finding acceptable places for cell towers and only zone those areas for their location. In that way, they are allowed per se, but only in areas zoned for it, much like industrial and commercial areas are zoned for specific locations. Those specified locations may not always be where companies would like them to be placed, but as long as the community has zoned for it, the community is protected from having them in other areas. If they are banned outright, then a successful court challenge by the company is likely, and cell towers would be able to be placed anywhere. Zoning allows for the needs of residents and the cell phone companies to be met in a fair and balanced way.

Open space can be protected when local governments partner with local organizations, as noted in the previous chapter. In so many areas of the country, developers try to purchase open space because it is ripe for lots of development. While many can debate whether or not development (i.e., the intensification of land use) is a good or bad thing, many members of towns think it would have a destructive impact on the local environment and adversely affect the character of the town. One way to protect open land from development is to purchase the land outright from owners and then rezone the property as recreational or undevelopable open space. Many county and state governments have set aside funds to help local communities purchase open space, and they are usually available as grants, where the local government has to be able to match that funding.

Part of the context of this approach to saving open space is that the land is privately owned. Whether the land is purchased or condemned by the local government, the property must be purchased at the market price. Since the expenditures for open space can be costly, there would be financial (and political) obstacles to use large sums of tax dollars to cover these costs. Local nonprofit organizations that are organized for the purpose of raising money for land acquisition would be the ideal partner for the local government. A local grassroots movement ensued to "save the farm" (the adopted name of the grassroots movement) from development. If enough money were going to be raised to purchase the property in this way, the new "owners" of the property would have to be the local government. In other words, its purchase would make the property become public property. Because of this arrangement, the local government would have to support this venture, even if no tax dollars were to be levied in the purchase of the property. Hence, a formal or informal partnership had to be maintained between the local government and the grassroots organizations.

A working farm in the town became available on the market at a time of major growth in the county. This property was seen as desirable among developers, but a number of residents wished to preserve the property as open space and started a grassroots organization to "save the farm" by seeking grants and other funding to raise the money to buy the property from the owners of the farm. If enough money were going to be raised to purchase the property in this way, the new "owners" of the property would have to be the local government. In other words, its purchase, though raised through a nonprofit organization, would make the property become public property. Because of this arrangement, the local government would have to support this venture, even if no tax dollars were to be levied in the purchase of the property. Hence, a formal or informal partnership had to be maintained between the local government and grassroots organizations.

In the case of the farm, enough money was raised to make a sizable down payment, but a mortgage was still needed. While some members of the grassroots movement were willing to use their own homes as collateral, the council still had to approve the arrangement. Some council members feared that there would be hidden government costs to this endeavor, and some may have had a philosophical bias against local government getting involved in such ventures. Nevertheless, a majority of council members agreed to work with the organization, and in time, the mortgage was paid off through fundraising. The farm has become an integral part of the community. The farm had served as an art colony for local artists, and many community events such as concerts, fairs and flea markets have been held there. It continues to have organic community gardens where residents can have their own plots. It has also been a source of recreation for residents in the town as well. Langhorne Open Space has continued to be a nonprofit organization that advocates the protection of open space and has worked with the Borough Council in other areas of town that needed to be preserved, through writing grant applications to county and state agencies for public monies to be used for other purchases of open space as well as other fundraising efforts.

While such a grassroots organization/government venture such as the example above can be highly successful, there are some important points that must be raised regarding it. First, in order to succeed, these endeavors require enough local government officials willing to support it. Second, and more importantly, there have to be residents in the community who can take leadership roles in moving the process along. These roles are not merely activist roles of organizing members of the community into a grassroots movement that advocates such a cause at different levels of government. It also must include individuals who can raise funds through grant writing and clever fund raising events. For the above case study, hundreds of thousands of dollars were raised through grants. Fairs, haunted house tours and art auctions were among the nongrant fundraising events. Communities thus need a talented base of people to embark upon such a project, and since they are not going to be paid for their efforts, they also need to have the types of jobs that allow sufficient flexibility to orchestrate these efforts. As a result, communities that have residents in professional occupations are more likely to pull off a venture like this. They have the talent, time, and the wherewithal to work with local, county and state officials. Having locally owned businesses that can also provide resources is also a bonus.

Such examples of the collaboration between the local government and the nonprofit organizations become a key way to address these kinds of issues, especially when the expenditure of large sums of money is involved. Local governments usually do not have the spare money laying around to purchase open space at the market value, yet through such a sale, the property will become public property owned by the municipality. Such a partnership requires trust among all parties involved as well as the willingness to be flexible when solving controversial issues.

LOW-INCOME HOUSING

Many communities seek to protect the property values of residents by enforcing zoning laws that inhibit low-income housing from being built. The goal is to maintain exclusivity and prevent certain types of houses from being built. Ordinances can also be passed to restrict the number of nonrelated people living in a household as a way to restrict group homes or members of lower social classes in the community. Partnerships with nonprofit organizations that serve needy populations the community does not necessarily want to in its backyards can also be discouraged. As noted previously, zoning is a strategy that local governments might employ to maintain social class and race homogeneity in their communities.

Providing opportunities for affordable housing can be one of the redistributive roles of local government (Yerena, 2015: 2). Yet, despite the growing need for low-income housing, local governments do not receive high grades for supporting efforts to create affordable housing (Silverman, 2009: 6). Indeed, there has been an ongoing shift from the public sector to the nonprofit sector as a way to address this problem of the lack of affordable housing (Silverman, 2009: 5). While most local government and nonprofit organization's attention to affordable housing has been addressed as neighborhood revitalization in low-income inner city areas (Fraser and Kick, 2007: 2357–2377), heterogeneous middle-class neighborhoods can also be part of this effort.

A countywide nonprofit organization works to secure home ownership for those who do not yet own a home approached government officials about providing home ownership opportunities for lower income families in the community. The organization generally purchases houses and then either sell them as individual homes, or in the case of a larger house, divides it into apartments or condominiums. The prices of these homes would be set below market value, which makes them more affordable for those with low incomes, and the reselling of these properties continues to be below market prices. The program plays a progressive role because housing costs have become so expensive, and many low and moderate-income families are shut out of the American dream of owning a home. Many communities, however, might not want to partner with such a nonprofit organization in order to be more exclusive in terms of the types of people living in their town. Residents in these communities would see the introduction of low and moderate-income families as having an adverse effect on property values.

The organization worked with a local church that had previously purchased several houses in the past to support their church-related activities. They worked with an interfaith housing organization to convert one of the houses into low-income housing condominiums. These condos would become available to families at prices well below the market value if they can meet eligibility requirements (based on low income). Local government assistance was needed because the property had to be rezoned for residential use. While the property was still classified as a nonprofit, and therefore exempt from taxes, services that are available to all residents of the town, at government expense, would be available to those who purchased their new condominiums. From that perspective, the housing structure would be no different from other residents in the town. However, other residents can argue that their property taxes are what pay for these services. At the suggestion of council, when the zoning changes were discussed, the church agreed to pay the equivalent of local property taxes each year to the town as a way to address these concerns. Such an agreement met the interests of both the nonprofit groups, allowing them to use the buildings, and of the borough. Since this arrangement was made solely between the town and the church, the tax-exempt status still applied to other taxes, such as the County and school district. This experience was not without problems once new residents moved into the new condominiums, but the experience is another example of how locally elected officials and nonprofit organizations can work together to address issues of common concern.

The decision of elected officials to work with nonprofit organizations cannot be viewed simply as a financial decision. It reflects the values of the town and the council members representing residents of the town. One can debate the benefits and drawbacks of working with nonprofit organizations. Should local government work to protect the image and subsequently the property values of the town? Is a more diversified community, consisting of people from various social classes and other situations a more meaningful community for residents? Citizens of each municipality have to make these decisions for themselves and elected officials should be conscious of them. However, these types of experiences can also show how "acting locally" can make a difference.

There are many good reasons for nonprofit organizations to make voluntary contributions to local government as part of this partnership. A lot of good will is generated from the donations, and a healthy relationship with the local municipality can only benefit the organization and its clients. Clients are residents of the town and interact with its tax-paying residents. Another benefit that nonprofit organizations can have working with the local municipality is when they have to work with local officials on special concerns, such special police coverage or a building permit. One cannot necessarily expect special favors that exempt the organization from local ordinances and regulations, but a good working relationship with the municipality can help speed up the processes up and government officials might be more receptive to discovering innovative ways to address their needs within the ordinance structure. Nonprofits can thus pose challenges for a local town, but the use of some basic common sense can make it a productive ongoing relationship that benefits all parties involved.

Some scholars refer to this model of cooperation as "collaborative management" that describes "the process of facilitating and operating in multiorganizational arrangements to solve problems that cannot be solved, or solved easily, by single organizations" (Agranoff and McGuire, 2003: 4). Such collaboration can be among government agencies, nonprofit organizations, granting institutions, among others. Relationships between elected officials and other organizations may need to develop over time, and philosophies of governing may need to be adjusted.

Another area that local government can play a progressive role concerns labor issues. Every municipality has a labor force. Even a small town will have a manager, secretary, building inspector, zoning officer, code enforcement officer, fire marshal, people working for the streets department and, of course, a police department. There is also the need for an attorney (the solicitor) and an engineer as well as someone to mow the grass in parks and retention basins. Larger towns will have even more positions, such as planners and health officers, among others.

Treatment of the labor force varies from municipality to municipality, and this treatment reflects the values of the people in charge, to a degree. While there has to be fiscal responsibility, how you pay the labor force becomes a political issue nonetheless. When parts of the labor force are organized in a union, negotiations become more formal. When there are no unions, wage increases for the next year can basically imposed on the labor force. Government officials need to keep costs down on behalf of the tax payers, but employees have bills to pay like everyone else and the financial exigencies of the town. While there would be some political pressure to pay employees as little as possible, in part to keep the need for tax increases under control, and in part for some elected officials to show the voters that they can be tough, such a strategy can also be "penny wise and pound foolish." Keeping a satisfied labor force means better work that is performed for the municipality, which can save money over the long run as you have an experienced and talented labor force to deal with the business of the town. In addition, paying your labor force fairly increases the likelihood of keeping good employees.

There are nonfinancial ways to put "politics in command" when working with one's labor force. Municipal employees can meet with the town's Personnel Committee over problems they encounter with their supervisors (who may even be other members of council). The process can be set up to be fair to all parties concerned and without fear of retribution by the supervisors. Instead of merely traditional annual reviews of employees by their supervisors and the Personnel Committee, annual dialogues can be set up as well where both the employees and their supervisors can share their views on what they see as problems facing the job at hand. This type of process seeks to reduce the apparent authority relationship that stems from a review of an employee's performance by giving employees the opportunity to also raise problems they see created by their supervisors. Such an arrangement gives more respect to labor, making it a two-way process, and the town's insurance costs were actually reduced because of this process. Such an arrangement may work better in a smaller town, though there are obstacles to implementing these kinds of arrangements. First, elected officials can be so busy trying to balance their paid day jobs with their government work and issues that are seen as non-pressing can be continuously put off. Second, specific problems that can emerge can often be handled as they came up in an informal manner, keeping the spirit of the original design intact. Third, when issues became adversarial that reflect divided elected members of government, these disputes tend to be addressed at official meetings. Unfortunately, when these disputes are raised in such a public forum, the press is there to cover all the details to be read by the public. While advocates of an employee may try to press the issue by making it public in a public meeting, this strategy hurts the employee in the long run. Once the newspapers cover the issue, it remains available on the internet for anyone, including prospective new employers of the employee to see.

When individuals run for local office, a common reason they give for seeking elective office is that they want to give something back to the community. It is certainly a laudable goal, and it certainly sounds better that saying one lusts for power or that one has a personal, self-serving agenda. Given the considerable time commitment of the job and the lack of pay commensurate to the time and effort put into the work, it does take a civic-minded person to add the demands of serving as a public servant to an already hectic life of managing a real job and family commitments. The important point is that holding elected office at the local level is a form of public service, and all elected officials have to serve willingly.

Depending on the structure of the local government, the mayor or the president of Council or Board, or chairperson of supervisors assumes the responsibility of chairing the meeting. Certain members of council and/or the mayor may prefer regularly scheduled public meetings be kept as short as possible. After all, meetings can go past midnight, and some members have to go to work the next day. While that is a goal for which one should strive, one has to consider what the consequences are for trying to make the meeting run as quickly as possible. One key consequence could be stifling public involvement in meetings. Council meetings are often well attended by local residents who either want to keep abreast of issues facing their town, or they may have a keen interest in a particular item on the agenda. The one chairing the meeting can either encourage or discourage public comment during deliberations. Obviously, the bigger the town, the more unwieldy the meeting can be and some controls have to be put in place. Indeed, school board meetings and larger townships must put time limits on public comment, otherwise meetings can get out of hand and last all night. However, one must weigh the consequences of limiting public involvement in discussion with savings of an extra hour. Allowing public input, without allowing any one person or group to monopolize the discussion, is a decision that makes the process more democratic and worth modest increases of time spent at a meeting. If one runs for office to "give something back to the community," then one should let that community be part of the political process to the extent to that is feasible.

CONCLUSION

There are many ways that local government officials can make a real difference in their community. Of course, one can make a difference simply by having the garbage collected properly in town, or by providing other key services as efficiently as possible. However, there are numerous areas where one can rely on their political values by helping the town in other meaningful ways. Preserving the environment is a global job, but much of the war is fought on the local level. If progressive people get involved in local government, part of that war can be won. The same case can be made for problems of housing, the financial problems that working people have in their daily lives, or even creating an environment that allows citizens to participate directly in the political process. One can be part of the solution. In conclusion, while there may not be a liberal or conservative way to pick up garbage, or a Republican or Democrat way to plow streets, there is a difference as to who holds elective office on the local level.

Chapter 4

Corruption . . . and Corruption "By Any Other Name"

There have been reports and studies of corruption at all levels of government, whether at the national, state or the local levels. However, it seems that residents are most likely to consciously connect corruption, nepotism, patronage and conflicts of interest at local levels of government than at higher levels of government. Despite knowing that highly paid corporate lobbyists enjoy unparalleled influence over elected officials in Washington, D.C. and that "big money interests" can influence the outcome of elections, most people have either grown accustomed to these phenomena or do not seem emotionally invested in it. And yet, citizens often associate local government with elected officials using local government for their own personal gain.

Citizens also tend to view police departments as appendages of local government. Enforcement of traffic infractions are attributed to monthly quotas imposed on police officers in order to support local government budgets. Enforcement of zoning laws, building codes (including acquiring the necessary building permits) and other local laws also are seen as unequally enforced, where elected officials are allowed to play by a different set of rules. This chapter examines the meanings, applications and nuances of corruption at the local level of government.

WHAT IS CORRUPTION?

The concept of corruption has taken on many meanings. Indeed, some say it has become little more than a way of disparaging government, or individuals within government that one does not like (Mendilow and Peleg, 2014: 1). Moreover, there can be nuances between what is considered corruption, and simply "sleaze." Some see corruption as actions that are blatantly illegal, and others include actions which, though legal, are immoral (a term too that can have multiple meanings, like someone who becomes corrupted due to securing a high-paying job for a company that pollutes the environment).

Corruption in government has a moral cost. It can undermine the legitimacy of government when it is felt that its actions benefit the interests of a few rather than the citizenry as a whole (Brogan, 2014: 158). If the public perceives that government can be bought, then the interests of the wealthy are seen as being represented more than others. Such an assumption undermines the credibility of local government and can discourage bright, committed and talented people from pursuing careers in public service, at least at the local level.

J.S. Nye defines corruption as "behavior which deviates from the formal duties of a public role" due to private financial or status gains or "violates rules against the exercise of certain types of private influence" (1967: 419). Included here are bribery ("the use of a reward to pervert the judgment of a person in a position of trust"); nepotism ("bestowal of a patronage by reason of a prescriptive relationship rather than merit"); or misappropriation ("illegal appropriation of public resources for private uses" (Nye, Ibid). Using Nye's well-quoted definition of corruption, the term applies only to "illegal activity" on the part of elected officials. Others see collecting bribes to receive permits, prohibiting competitors from entry into the area through ordinances and creative enforcement of existing ordinances (Shleifer and Vishnny, 1993: 599).

"Market-centered" definitions focus on public officials who enjoy pecuniary gains according to availability of supply and demand in the market place of their jurisdictions (Werner, 1983: 147). Moreover, some consider betrayal of the public interests as corruption (Werner, ibid). However, this type of cultural definition may or may not constitute illegal forms of corruption. An elected official whose behavior may not be necessarily in tune with the interests of one's constituents, or whose votes or actions may not be considered in the public interest, may not necessarily be corrupt in the way Nye defines it. Elected officials are elected to represent their constituencies, and they can say they sometimes have to make the proverbial "tough decisions" that can be construed as contrary to the interests of constituents. While maybe not illegal, the consequences of these kinds of actions become issues later on when elected officials run for re-election.

Others identify corruption as the subversion of the public interest or common good to the interests of private interests (Philip, 1997: 441). Of course, anyone who follows politics has seen some examples of elected and/or appointed officials who equate the interests of private interests to the public interest, particularly, although not exclusively, when it concerns increased development in a local area. Even the use of public money for the construction of a baseball stadium to be used by a privately owned team is couched as a good investment for the geographic area as a whole (Cagan and deMause,

1998: 33–35). Sometimes, support for the private sector can take place, even when referring to the private interest of a single company. For example, is a town better off when a cable company constructs a system of wiring in a town, even though it means one cable company will then have the monopoly in that area? Hence, what constitutes public versus private interests can only be understood within a political context.

Others have noted that corruption can include the "diversion and outright theft of funds for public programs and damage caused by firms and individuals that pay bribes to avoid health and safety regulations intended to benefit the public (Svensson, 2005: 19). Selling government, or public property, embezzlement and/or receiving kickbacks in public procurement would fall into this category. For those companies engaged in the practice of bribing officials, these costs would be seen as a tax, or fee for doing business" (Svensson, 2005: 20).

While one might consider elected officials succumbing to lobbying as a form of corruption, there are some important distinctions between lobbying and corruption. First, bribery is considered illegal activity that includes giving money or something else of value to a public official with the corrupt intent to directly influence an action of that official (Teachout, 2014: 216). Bribery is illegal while lobbying is not. Second, bribery is usually specific to a firm, while the impact of lobbying usually affects all businesses within a specific industry or trade (Svensson, 21). One should note, however, that while there may be a consensus in the United States that bribery is a clear-cut form of corruption, and indeed a criminal offense, attitudes about bribery are by no means universal (Philp, 1997: 442–444).

Though lobbying is not seen as illegal, it still gives to some groups much more influence in government decision making, and the laws and rules that regulate lobbying may have been made by elected officials who have been unduly influenced by lobbyists who would have been greatly affected by such rules. Moreover, as long as substantial campaign contributions remain legal, there is a blurry line between buying influence and supporting candidates with similar political philosophies, and can be a potential threat to representative democracies. That is, lobbying can shift from being a "civic wrong to a First Amendment right" (Teachout, 2014: 6). The 2010 Supreme Court case regarding *Citizens United* "effectively gave wealthy individuals and wealthy corporations the right to spend as much money as they want in their efforts to influence elections and policy" (Teachout, 2014:7).

Burke has long noted that corruption can mean undue influence over certain groups and exercising arbitrary power that is not anchored in any system (Mendilow and Peleg, 2014: 9–10). However, corruption laws and regulations react to shifting realities. As a consequence, what is considered to be corruption can only be discussed within a specific sociopolitical context. Recent outrage over the Supreme Court's *Citizens United* decision also demonstrates the lack of a clear social and legal consensus on this issue; definitions of corruption or undue influence of government officials have to be decided politically or by the courts.

CORRUPTION IN GOVERNMENT

Much of the scholarly literature on corruption has often been applied to discussions of governments in countries in the Third World, or underdeveloped countries. As these countries became increasingly integrated into the world capitalist economy, their economies and infrastructure needed to "modernize" in order to accommodate this modernization process. Indeed, corruption has been seen as associated with the very process of modernization, whether this process took place more than one hundred years ago in the Western countries or in underdeveloped countries in Asia, Africa or South America more recently (Werner, 1983: 147). Given the lack of development, and the groups that benefited economically and politically from premodernization, some form of catalyst was viewed as necessary in order to overcome the structural, political and cultural barriers preventing a country from moving forward. Corruption was seen as promoting economic development, cutting red tape, overcoming divisions within a ruling elite, incentivizing that elite, overcoming discrimination against minority groups and integrating talented non-elites into modern life (Nye, 1967: 419–421).

When the level of social inequality is high, incentives for using corruption for personal gain is also high. States that are poorer and less educated are more likely to be corrupt and have a poor foundation for democracy (Glaeser and Saks, 2005:1055; Smith, 1996:165). Moreover, as income and education levels rise within a population, there is greater citizen involvement in politics (Glaesner and Saks, 1056). As a result, corruption will have taken place as countries modernize, in part as a way to overcome economic and political barriers to economic growth, and as a means of social mobility for government officials who can use their political status for self-benefit. Moreover, the less educated and poorer the population the less is the ability of the mass population to monitor such corruption.

Others have argued that increased inequality actually creates the conditions necessary for corruption.

> As income inequality increases, the rich have more to lose through fair political, administrative, and judicial processes. With the increased inequality, the rich also have greater resources that can be used to buy influence, both legally and illegally. (You and Khagram, 2005: 138)

Corruption, according to this approach becomes a normal part of the political landscape at all levels of government as a way to produce policy outcomes that favor the smaller numbers of wealthy individuals at the expense of the masses. Where a government is situated along the federal to local continuum can be seen as important as well. Indeed You and Khagram indicate that contrary to assumptions held by most political analysts, smaller levels of government tend to experience greater amounts of corruption (2005: 154).

Elected officials at all levels of government have been convicted of various forms of corruption, though the numbers of convictions varies from year to year (Goel and Nelson, 1998: 114). However, while state-level as well as federal convictions seemed to have stabilized in the 1980s, Goel and Nelson reported that convictions at local levels of government continued to rise more or less steadily (1998: 109).

While the United States undoubtedly has experienced corruption throughout its history, forms of corruption remain part of its political and cultural landscape today. Those who take bribes will take them for their own personal financial incentives. While some may offer bribes for preferential treatment (what economists call "government rents") such as being awarded government contracts, others may do so as a means to cut through red tape. The profits to be made in the intensification of land use (housing and commercial development) and in use of real estate can be quite large, enough to justify companies bribing government officials.

Desirable government actions sought by developers and other business interests might include zoning changes and exceptions to allow development, subdivision approvals, building permits, among others (Amick, 1976: 77). Such lobbying can lead to the relaxation of certain ordinances or codes in individual cases. Uneven enforcement of various ordinances and codes is a criticism often made by the public at government meetings, echoing the sentiments noted earlier on corruption at the local level. Since this type of discrepancy in enforcement is easily seen by residents, these sentiments get reinforced.

Conflicts of interest occur when elected or appointed government officials make decisions in an official capacity that improve one's own personal economic fortunes (Amick 1976: 106). For example, an elected official may secretly own land that subsequently gets rezoned to increase its value, without recusing oneself from the decision-making process. Usually one is expected to make one's conflict of interest known at a public meeting, and the issue of recusing oneself from decision making is often what it expected. Amick notes that this kind of corruption tends to take place when the official is part-time as opposed to being a career full-time public servant (Ibid). Part-time officials tend to draw their primary source of income from another job. This phenomenon can relate to government officials at local levels of government, who tend to be part-time volunteers serving their communities, or attorneys, engineers or other professionals who are hired part-time due to their unique expertise that is needed by the town. Many of these part-timers are also elected officials. There is no real notion of career service in local government; elected officials come and go as their positions are secondary to their full-time professions. Since they usually do not intend to remain in office for a long time, developing a legacy or record of accomplishments and acting in the general interest of the population as a whole is not the same as it is at higher levels of government, or for those individuals who indeed have ambitions to run for higher office.

For example, if an elected board or council needed to raise taxes, and most of the decision makers were retired and living off social security and/or pensions, they could opt for an earned income tax, a policy that would not impact them, and yet, would accomplish the needed increase in government revenues. They might opt for this remedy rather than an increase in property taxes that they would have to pay as well. After such a vote, even if the results are strongly unpopular with the public, one usually does not have long-term plans to stay in office so there is less concern with being held accountable at the next election.

Nepotism is another form of government corruption, though not without controversy and debate. Nepotism, like corruption in general, has been defined differently over time. Most view nepotism as involving favoritism when hiring relatives of key employees or officials as well as having relatives in supervisory, executive or policy-making decisions (Ewing, 1965: 23). The boundaries of nepotism can vary. While most would include spouses and children (and their spouses) within the category of people to be included for nepotism purposes, the degree to which nephews and nieces, first cousins, and distant relatives are included in this category is open to interpretation. The problem of hiring members of one's family, regardless of how one determines the boundaries of family, has become complicated because of changing economic realities. With more families requiring two incomes and an increasingly tight job market for everyone including one's children, there is pressure to help family members. Moreover, the public sector is growing as an area of employment, which makes the issue of nepotism particularly relevant (Podgers, 1996: 2).

The practice of nepotism raises many problems for local governments. Showing favoritism when hiring relatives as employees of government can deny better qualified candidates from employment and perhaps doing the job better. The practice of nepotism can therefore compromise the quality of the services provided to the public. Moreover, when the public recognizes that family members of either elected officials or key officials are hired, the image of local government becomes tainted. The practice merely confirms for many the belief that local government is corrupt and that you have to "know somebody or be a relative" to get a position. Besides, the negative image that nepotism gives to the public, applications for future openings may be reduced because of the perception that one will not get the position anyway due to past practice. The consequence once again, would be a smaller pool of applicants, where more qualified applicants are discouraged from applying.

While the problems of nepotism apply at all levels of government, as well as within the private sector, there are additional problems associated with nepotism in local government. Elected officials may not necessarily be a united group when discussing possible laws, ordinances and codes for the town. Often, there are disagreements, conflicts of philosophy, and the normal disputes that occur at every level of government. While elected officials at state and federal levels have research staffs to support their efforts, local government officials, especially in smaller towns and municipalities, all share a common staff. Because "knowledge is often power" when it comes to charting the waters of contested matters in local government, nepotism can create an imbalance that favors those with information. Loyalty to specific elected officials can lead to an imbalance in the distribution of important information needed to help make policy. Moreover, nepotism can contribute to cliquishness among elected and appointed officials, which also leads to government becoming a less productive and efficient entity.

On the other hand, there are criticisms of anti-nepotism laws as well. Sometimes, a spouse could be the most qualified person, and banning nepotism prevents the local government from hiring a very desirable candidate. Sometimes, qualified candidates may be hard to find.

> The most blatant use of nepotism—spouse hiring spouse, sibling hiring sibling—tend to obscure the fact that much of the time, this is a difficult issue, especially in small towns where the pool of available talent is small anyway. (Ehrenhalt, 2001: 8)

While one does not want to have a lesser qualified person hired in a government position because of family ties to elected officials or key appointed position holders, denying the most qualified person from serving in a position because of their family relationship does not make sense either. In some cases, people have become romantically involved with someone they work with and subsequently marry. Would one of the married couple now have to leave as a penalty for marrying someone they met at work? (Podgers, 1996: 2).

Another problem with anti-nepotism laws is that legitimate family traditions can be threatened or destroyed (Ehrenhalt, 2001: 8). There are families that have a tradition for generations of working for the fire company or the police. Sons have followed their fathers, their siblings followed siblings, and employment in these areas constituted a form of family pride and solidarity more than a vehicle for material gain (Poders, Ibid). Many simply go into a line of work because a relative inspired them to do so. As a result, some have advocated that anti-nepotism laws should somehow accommodate children following in the footsteps of a family member (Carden, 2012: 2). Of course, proponents of anti-nepotism laws could say that hiring family members under this pretext can also prevent better qualified unrelated candidates from securing positions.

Case Study

There are many positions that have to be filled in local government, including building inspectors, code enforcement officers, a zoning officer, street maintenance workers, police officers, office secretary and someone to mow the grass on municipal land. In the case of lawn mowing, the son of a member of council had a landscaping business. He was interested in the mowing contract. If having to deal with employees who are also neighbors can be difficult, try to consider what it is like when the applicant for a job is the spouse or child of an elected official! Handling this potential problem was easy as the bid for mowing was advertised and all the bids were opened at a public meeting. The son of a member of council was the lowest bid and won the contract fair and square. An anti-nepotism law in this case would have resulted in the town having to pay more for the same mowing service.

Hiring building inspectors and code enforcement officers can be trickier. Expertise can vary and the pay for the positions is fixed. It is desirable in many ways to hire someone from your town as it keeps the money in your town and that person is a known commodity. On the other hand, a local resident will have friends in town, and one has to worry about uneven enforcement of the ordinances and codes in order to accommodate friends. Even people working for the streets department can favor the cleaning of streets in one part of town over the other. Such favoritism might be seen as a petty form of corruption, but it is still a form of corruption nonetheless. The best way to control for such a problem is to assure oversight of employees to make sure they treat everyone as equally as possible.

Most municipalities prefer to fill local jobs with local people—individuals who reside within their boundaries. Some municipalities require it, especially for police.

This kind of policy certainly can work in an urban area, or even a big town, but in smaller communities it may be difficult to impose such a residency requirement. One argument in favor of hiring locally is the fact that these jobs are paid out of tax dollars collected from residents in the town. The local resident is more likely to support local businesses in the town. Hiring from among the pool of residents in effect keeps money within the town.

At the same time there are some obvious drawbacks to hiring local people. Everyone in town interacts with town employees as neighbors, friends, someone you see at back to school night. When people do their job satisfactorily, everything goes smoothly and everyone is happy. However, when there are concerns about the competence of an employee, and they reside in town, handling the situation becomes more complicated, especially in smaller towns where everyone knows most people. As a consequence, any official interaction with the employee that has to do with concerns about how well the job is getting done can become a public matter. Moreover, any disciplinary action, including having to fire someone, can become embarrassing to the employee, who must continue facing one's neighbors long after the action is taken.

Case Study

When employees of the town are in a position to show partiality toward other residents in town, this can become problematic. Irate residents wanted to know why their streets weren't plowed after a big snowstorm, while the street where the employee lived was done early and thoroughly. While this type of situation could be construed as abuse, it is more of a petty complaint. As long as all the streets get done, there should not be a problem. Obviously, main streets should be plowed before small side streets; while some may consider this type of favoritism a form of corruption this is obviously not a serious abuse of power.

If the employee is a Building Inspector, or a Zoning Officer, then partiality or incompetence can be lead to more serious problems. As noted previously, the zoning book is where the community lays the ground rules that shape how development in town should take place. This includes, for example, how far a building can be from someone else's property, how many additional units, if any, can be in a house or building, and many other directives that aim to maintain the character of the town and protect neighbors from anything too extreme being built next door. The Zoning Officer is there to uphold these rules. The building codes are there to ensure that construction or remodeling is done "up to code" to assure the safety of current and future residents. This includes anything from electrical work and plumbing to how deep concrete should be set on driveways and sidewalks. The Building Inspector is in charge of enforcing these rules. The persons who fill these positions make lasting impacts on the quality of life in town. When work is done poorly or in the case of uneven application of standards, they can do a great deal of damage. It is great when everything works as it should, but it is difficult when there are personnel problems. In such a case, one needs to deal with not only the problems of uneven enforcement or the regulations or worse—potential incompetence—but also the impacted resident, who has friends and neighbors in town.

Careful thought must accompany the hiring of local residents for local government posts. Giving a job to a resident is preferable to one who is not a taxpayer to the town. Yet calls of "favoritism" or corruption will often follow such an appointment. In order for this type of arrangement to work, the person has to be clearly competent and qualified for the job. Having someone who is well respected by others in town is an additional plus. Making sure you have hired qualified, responsible candidates whose integrity is beyond reproach is the best way to avoid potential problems.

CORRUPTION BY ANY OTHER NAME

There is no controversy in recognizing that bribery is a form of corruption, and most consider nepotism, at least to some degree, to be corruption as well. When there are competing interests in local government with regard to a town's policies and rulings and consequently—winners and losers, and ways to potentially skirt the rules—there become opportunities for "corruption by any other name."

One example of "corruption by any other name" is the idea of gifting. That is, elected or appointed officials may be given gifts that are not necessarily tied to a request to act in a particular way. Concerns over gifting government officials as a possible form of corruption goes back to the times of Benjamin Franklin, who was given very valuable gifts from King Louis XVI when Franklin completed his post as Ambassador to France and was returning back to the United States (Teachout, 2014: 1–5). While imparting gifts to foreign diplomats once they completed their service was a common custom in Europe, that very same act was seen as buying influence or loyalties in the United States. Such debate continues to this day. They include tangible items as well as less tangible gifts like campaign donations that are, in essence, financial gifts to an elected official. The Supreme Court's recent ruling on *Citizens United* is only part of this ongoing debate. The Supreme Court ruled that unlimited campaign contributions which give excessive influence to big money groups does not violate the law. Indeed, the deciding vote in the decision was cast by Justice Kennedy who ruled that for campaign contributions to be illegal, there must be "explicit exchange for something of value for a specific, identifiable legislative or executive act" (Teachout, 2014: 7). At the state level, elected officials, such as governors, are allowed to receive gifts, but they must be publicly acknowledged. In other words, giving gifts to officials is not illegal, and is thus not a form of corruption, *per se*. The degree to which such gift giving, whether in material goods or in financial contributions, gives one influence over elected or appointed officials is not fully addressed by such laws and rulings. But even though it is legal, is it nonetheless still a form of corruption?

Providing gifts by appointed professionals and/or individuals who have some relationship to elected officials in local government without a specific *quid pro quo* request for a reciprocal favor is legal and common. On one level, it can be seen as a token of appreciation for being selected to perform services already performed, and on the other, there is a culture of gift giving, especially during the holiday season. However, common sense suggests that when gifts are bestowed upon elected officials, those elected officials who chose to accept the gifts are somewhat compromised in future independent deliberations on issues that impact these affected parties. Since these individuals have to be rehired by the very same people who received the gifts, evaluations of their previous work might be compromised.

Case Study

In December of my first years as an elected member of council, I answered the door and the delivery person handed me a big box with a Honeybaked Ham in it. There was a note inside that simply said "Happy Holidays" from the town's engineer. At the next Council meeting, the solicitor gave each member of council a very nice package of gourmet cookies, also with a note commemorating the holiday season.

Since these professionals are hired by the council, and it was the holiday season, which is a normal time for gift giving, they were undoubtedly in the holiday spirit and may have wanted to show their appreciation for being hired by the council for their services. The expenditure was probably even a business deduction as well.

These professionals, however, were to be reappointed the following month. Does receiving gifts a month before influence the judgment of council members when deciding whether or not to renew the services of professionals at the January meeting? No one will say it does, but it has to have some impact.

After becoming council president, we established a policy that paid professionals could not give gifts to elected officials. This policy was amended as the solicitor made donations to charities in the name of the council, and this did not seem to put members of council in a potential conflict of interest when considering whether to maintain the solicitor for the following year. At least, elected officials received no material gift of any kind.

There is certainly nothing illegal about paid professionals hired by local government giving gifts to town officials. While you do not hear about gift giving at the local level, you likely would with a governor, whose receipt of gifts can make national news. There is no question that such a practice affords some influence, and having disclosure rules or laws only makes the gift giving public; it does not ban the practice of their possible effects.

A corollary of such tangible gift giving to elected officials is campaign contributions. Financial contributions to candidates running for office are necessary for candidates to be competitive and have long been a part of our political system. Campaign contributions are often where "corruption by any other name," though legal, in local government can be found (Boyarsky and Boyarsky (1974: 63). As noted in chapter 2, conflict at the local level between the "growth machine" and local residents who oppose intensification of land use is a major problem. Developers, real estate companies, attorneys, and other beneficiaries of increased growth and development in their area are often important sources of campaign contributions to candidates running for elected office. Perhaps they are supporting candidates who share their view that the town needs more development. They are in sync with the needs of the "growth machine."

Campaign contributions are legal, and contributors may simply be donating to candidates running for office who share their philosophy with regard to development in the area. Candidates running for office or re-election to office may adopt positions that are pro-development because contributions from wealthy sectors of the area may then make possible financial contributions to their campaign. Either way, the campaign structure, based on donations, usually gives benefits to those with money, which translates then to more lawn signs, more mailings to residents, newspaper and/or television ads, and even get out the vote ground games. These candidates have a greater chance of winning because of their expanded war chest and pro-development views may thus prevail in local government. There is a considerable body of research that documents the influence of moneyed interests in shaping local government policy (e.g., Teachout, 2014; Boyarsky and Boyarsky, 1974; Hanrahan, 1977; Amick, 1976). Is this illegal? Obviously not. Is it corruption? It depends on how corruption is defined. There is no specific direct financial payoff for a specific policy, but is the interest of the public compromised by vested interests? Does the shift in one's political views attributable to receipt of campaign contributions give vested interests significant influence in political decisions? Probably so. But it is legal. And with the *Citizens United* decision, the Supreme Court has allowed for much more money to be given to candidates. While legal, it does potentially give increasing influence to interests with deeper pockets. This legal "gift giving" can be seen as "corruption by another name."

As noted in chapter 2, a principal form of conflict at the local level concerns intensification of land use. The "growth machine" which consists of developers, the local real estate industry, trade unions and their allies influence local government to support development projects. Support for pro-development policies is a way for local politicians to reward those who give political donations and support the political party over time. This reciprocity has been called patronage. Patronage is also relevant when examining corruption in local government. Governments increasingly "outsource" functions and activities previously performed by employees of the local government. The above case study talks about soliciting bids for mowing municipally owned land and fields. At one point, employees of the town did this job. According to research by Lobao, Adua and Hooks (2014: 66) privatization policies have been adopted at an increasing rate by local governments with greater administrative capacity and a larger unionized workforce.

Patronage is also relevant when examining corruption in local government through the transition to the privatization of government functions. This refers to functions and tasks normally and previously performed by government bodies but "outsourced" to the private sector. Privatization has been defined as "market-oriented government that elevates private interests over collective public interests" (Lobao, Adua and Hooks, 2014: 644) or the attainment of a public policy goal by relying on the private sector (Greene, 199: 17). The use of privatization is a debate that takes place at all levels of government: whether to achieve public goals through the merits of positive government actions and responsibilities or the virtues of capitalism and free markets (Greene, Ibid: 17). Some functions of government, at least for small towns, have been privatized for quite a while, such as garbage collection and water systems, because private companies have the economies of scale to provide cheaper service by contracting out to several municipalities. Thereby, the cost of machinery can be shared among more than one town. These assumptions, however, have been called into question by researchers studying the impact of privatization on solid waste and water services (Bel, Fageda and Warner, 2010: 553–577).

There is a certain appeal for local governments to want to contract out services that were once "in house." It is taken for granted that private businesses can do the government's work more efficiently, better and cheaper (Hanrahan, 1977: 2). Researchers have documented these savings (Bennett and DiLorenzo, 1983: 33–45). The thinking is that government officials are not using their own personal money and are not personally financially responsible for any inefficient use of government funds and waste has a history of being a feature of government-run activities. Private companies, on the other hand, have to be responsible for the money spent, and as a result should give greater attention to efficiencies of the operation.

There is intuitive appeal to such a partnership between governments at all levels with the private sector. The saving of money is obviously important. Moreover, an important cultural value—part of the ideology, that pervades the United States—is that government should be limited and the private sector should be left unfettered. Such a value is consistent with government relying on the private sector for services. But practice is not always consistent with this theoretical set of assumptions.

There is also an intuitive value in putting out contracts for bid for services or construction for a local government. Unlike negotiations, which gives the government official some discretion in selecting a private company as well as settling on a price, the bidding process makes certain that everyone has an equal chance to be awarded the contract. The process certainly has the appearance of being fair and above board, and it usually is. Specifications for the type of construction or services are made public for everyone to bid, and since all firms are bidding on the same specifications, one can take the lowest bid. Amick lists various ways; however, this theoretically competitive process can be undermined. These include barring would-be bidders because they are not found to be qualified (Amick, 1976: 16). Officials could comment that potential bidders received negative evaluations from other municipalities. Specifications could be specifically designed to give a particular bidder an advantage, and bidders can make unrealistically low bids to be awarded the contract, and then lobby for costly changes along the way that are later approved by a government official (Amick, Ibid). All bids could be rejected for various reasons, such as that all bids were higher than expected or even some technical matter (Amick, Ibid).

Hanrahan has indicated that this partnership between the private sector and local government "has harmed many state and local governments through inflated contracts, leasing arrangements, franchises and concessions" as well as special tax breaks (1977: 6). His research found numerous instances of bid-rigging. Moreover, a company may win a contract with the lowest bid, only to follow up with cost overruns and/or cut the level of service promised. The assumption that the work of the private sector is cheaper than government-run services have been called into question by researchers studying the impact of privatization on solid waste and water services (Bel, Fageda and Warner, 2010: 553–577).

There are reasons to resist the temptation to privatize or outsource what were previously tasks performed by local government. There is a profit motive that private companies must have in order to stay in business, and that profit has to be built into what is charged to local governments. Governments do not have to make a profit when providing services or building roads, for example. Companies that provide services to governments hire their own employees. While this practice certainly helps the local government's bookkeeping functions, because what was once a labor force that had to have wages and salaries along with the appropriate deductions calculated, now is reduced to one line on a budget. However, there is little control over wages paid by these companies. Their profit motive may encourage them to hire cheaper labor and provide little or no benefits. This practice would then tend to perpetuate a cycle where the wages and salaries of the labor force fail to keep up with the cost of living. The power of government employees' unions can be weakened by contracting out work normally done by employees of the local government, bypassing civil service regulations such as giving preference to veterans, or affirmative action procedures (Sharkansky, 1980: 117).

Moreover, the potential impact of connections, the awarding of contracts due to patronage, and the vulnerability of governments to have to adhere to guidelines of the contracts with private companies, does not lead to an open and fair playing field. Conflicts of interest have been seen as a "frequent companion of contracting" (Sharkansky, 1980: 119). Hence, while theoretically intuitive that privatization can be the best financial deal for local governments the opposite consequences can be the result. The inescapable conclusion is that contracting out, far from being a potential boon for state and local governments, is a major source of corruption, financial waste and inefficiency. In many cases it is a major cause of local governments' fiscal problems (Hanrahan, 1977: 3). Because of potential overruns, overcharges, lack of inspection when inferior products are used, local governments can end up paying more money for less efficiently run services.

CONCLUSION

While there is no clear consensus as to what the boundaries of corruption might be, there is general agreement that an elected official who takes bribes or uses one's positions for one's direct personal gain is corruption, actions that are considered illegal. There is, however, an important gray area when one considers the subversion of the public interest for private purposes. There are reasons for concern in an era where political campaign contributions are a ubiquitous feature of politics at all levels of government, and those contributions come with an expectation, or at least the hope that those contributions will translate into government actions beneficial to the giver. As long as there are "winners" and "losers" with regard to government actions, the gray area of corruption or the normal operation of politics will continue.

Conclusion

Local governments have to perform many of the same functions provided at higher levels of government. Basic services have to be provided to residents, including maintaining a police force for public safety, monitoring construction to make sure building codes are followed, and passing ordinances regarding zoning, development and the environment. Naturally, there will be variations in the size and scope of local governmental responsibilities based on the population and geography of each town and its unique properties.

One theme that has been pervasive throughout the book is that the actions of local government, like those at national and state levels, are not void of political conflict due to competing interests. There are winners and losers in most actions that local government takes. As a consequence, competing groups become active in order to have more influence and to make sure their interests are articulated in policies. Some groups have more assets and resources than others and, as a result, have more influence.

For example, all levels of government have fiduciary responsibilities to their taxpayers. Budgeting allows for the most efficient way of using tax dollars efficiently. Such a process does not at face value appear to be one that represents a potential conflict of interests. However, as with most aspects of government, the nature of taxation and expenditures involves political processes. How one chooses to both collect taxes and spend money is decided politically, and there are winners and losers based on the decisions that are made. Some groups may end up paying proportionally more or less based on these decisions. At the local level of government, for example, property taxes are a chief source of providing income for government. Property taxes are a progressive form of taxation, because those with higher valued homes will be required to pay a higher property tax. These taxes can then be used to support education as well as all the other services that the local government provides.

There have been efforts to modify the way taxes are collected, including the creation of an "earned income tax (EIT)." On one level the EIT is also a progressive tax, because the more income an individual makes, the more they pay. Senior citizens—who normally have less earned income—would not have to pay increasingly higher property taxes. However, such a tax does not include "unearned" income, such as social security payments, dividends or sales from stocks and other investments, and pensions. The more wealthy people are, the more likely their income can come from investments that would not be considered to be earned income. As a result, some retired people with high levels of income from pensions, social security and private investments would not be required to pay any tax from this income. However, working families with lower incomes would have to pay this new kind of tax. It is clear that decisions regarding how taxes are collected have "winners" and "losers" even though the consequences of such policies may or may not be intentional.

As noted in chapter 2, the main locus of conflict at the local governmental level is over growth, or the intensification of land use. Intensification of land use replaces open space with more homes, shopping centers and other features of development that pit the economic interests of the growth machine that leads to increased growth against those of residents and local businesses wanting to preserve the environment and maintain the existing residential character of the town. In these conflicts, coalitions are not divided strictly along class lines. As noted, organized labor, at least that part which is connected to the building trades, help make up "the growth machine" that is in favor of increased development.

These conflicts at the local level get articulated within the workings of local government. Zoning ordinances, regulations regarding the environment, including the definition and maintenance of wetlands and open space, and other types of local laws embody these conflicts. These ordinances set the rules or framework for residential and commercial development in the local area, and can be construed as either pro-growth or attempts to regulate such development.

Some community residents want to prevent new development altogether. As a result, there are "winners and losers" in the outcomes of local governmental actions as they relate to development, which compels both "the growth machine" and residents to be politically engaged in local government. And where residents are not part of the political process, the interests of developers often prevail. At the same time, "victories" against the growth machine by organized residents can also have the effect (intended or not) of maintaining social class and at times, the racial exclusivity and homogeneity of the community.

Elected officials can also make a difference in addressing larger social issues. While many social issues such as climate change go beyond the ability of local governments to solve, "acting locally" is a key place to begin to address such issues. By addressing issues such as how municipalities get their electricity or how they go about recycling, for example, are ways local governments can play a role in being a part of the larger solution. Decisions such as purchasing renewable sources of energy for the town, recycling and other similar measures can be ways local governments can contribute to the solution of larger environmental problems.

Issues regarding economic inequality and social justice are also opportunities where local government officials can make an impact. How local governments choose to deal with low-income housing and even the treatment of local employees reflect certain values in the decision-making process. For example, providing low-income housing may help solve the larger problem of providing more fair housing options. And some residents see value in having an integrated town, across social classes. Other residents may prefer the homogeneity of one's neighborhood as a way to preserve (or perceived to preserve) property values in the town, or simply to preserve an economically homogeneous population in town. Hence, there are "winner and losers" again when local government decisions are made in these areas.

A second theme present throughout the book is that at the local level there are hidden ways that vested economic interests are maintained. For example, the phenomenon of "taxes by any other name" is one way governments can increase taxes in less traditional and less transparent ways.

As noted in chapter 4 on corruption, business interests and professionals, looking to secure appointed contracts or positions with the local government, can try to influence local government officials. Some types of influence, such as bribery, are clearly illegal and there are numerous instances of charges of corruption made against local government officials. However, there is also "corruption by another name," which can involve more discreet ways to obtain influence or secure contracts. Although local governments try to prevent such practices by establishing ground rules that are fair for everyone and help prevent unfair competition, these practices cannot always prevent an uneven playing field in hiring professionals to help local government officials as well as in giving out contracts for work.

Because many decisions made by local government officials impact different sectors of the population differently, residents who stay engaged with the workings of their local governments are in a better position to oversee these practices. An informed citizenry is the best check on government actions. Moreover, their active engagement can help shape decision making by government officials in ways that are consistent with their interests. As noted in the previous chapters, business interests participate in the local political process by lobbying, contributing to campaigns or through active membership in the local political parties. Residents are less likely to stay as engaged in the workings of local government, as it takes extra volunteer work on their part. However, the lack of residential involvement can lead to decisions that are contrary to their interests and vision for the town.

Active participation by residents can provide a watchdog effect on the operations of local government to make sure that elected officials are using government resources fairly and efficiently. Active participation can be a check to ensure that forms of corruption do not take place. An engaged and active population also serves as a counterforce to business interests. Active, engaged citizens can also steer elected officials to take initiatives that solve problems, such as preserving open space, protecting the environment, treating all groups in town fairly and equally, and addressing problems perpetuated by increasing inequality. A democracy prospers when there is such engagement; decision making by elected officials then has to take the needs and interests of concerned residents into account.

Bibliography

Aaron, H. (1974, May). A New View pf Property Tax Incidence. *The American Economic Review, 64*(2), 212–221.

Agranoff, R., & McGuire, M. (2003). *Collaborative Public Management: New Strategies for Local Government.* Washington, DC: Georgetown University Press.

Amick, G. (1976). *The American Way of Graft.* Princeton, NJ: The Center of Analysis of Public Issues.

Baldassare, M. (1992). Suburban Communities. *Annual Review of Sociology, 18,* 475–494.

Beauregard, R. A. (2001). Federal Policy and Postwar Urban Decline: A Case of Government Complicity?, *Housing Policy Debate, 12*(1), 129–151.

Beauregard, R. A. (2006). *When America Became Suburban.* Minneapolis: University of Minnesota Press.

Been, V. (2010, Winter). Community Benefits Agreements: A New Local Government Tool or Another Variaiton on the Exactions Theme? *The University of Chicago Law Review, 77*(1), 5–35.

Beeri, I., & Navot, D. (2013). Local Political Corruption. *Public Management Review, 15*(5), 712–739. Retrieved from http://dx.doi.org/10.1080/14719037.2012.707682

Bel, G., Fageda, X., & Warner, M. E. (2010, Summer). Is Private Production of Public Services Cheaper than Public Production? A Meta-Regression Analysis of Solid Waste and Water Services. *Journal of Policy Analysis and Management, 29*(3), 553–577.

Bennett, J. T., & DiLorenzo, T. J. (1983, Winter). Public Employee Unions and the Privatization of "Public" Services. *Journal of Labor Research, IV*(1), 33–35.

Bernstein, M. H. (1972, July). Ethics in Government: The Problems in Perspective. *National Civic Review, 61*(7), 341–347.

Bowen, W. M., Salling, M. J., Haynes, K. E., & Cyran, E. J. (1995, December). Toward Environmental Justice: Spatial Equity in Ohio and Cleveland. *Annals of the Association of American Geographers, 85*(4), 641–663.

Boyarsky, B., & Boyarsky, N. (1974). *Backroom Politics: How Your Local Politicians Work, Why Your Local Government Doesn't and What You Can Do About It.* Los Angeles: J. P. Tarcher, Inc.

Brogan, M. (2014). Corruption Competition: Local Power Nodes, Corruption, and Sleaze. In J. Mendilow & I. Peleg, *Corruption in the Contemporary World* (pp. 153–172). Lanhan, MD: Lexington Books.

Bruegman, R. (2005). *Sprawl: A Compact History*. Chicago: University of Chicago Press.

Burawoy, M. (2005). The Critical Turn to Public Sociology. *Critical Sociology, 31*(3), 313–331.

Burchell, R. W., Downs, A., McCann, B., & Mukherji, S. (2005). *Sprawl Costs: Economic Impacts of Unchecked Development*. Washington, DC: Island Press.

Christensen, T., & Hogen-Esch, T. (2006). *Local Politics: A Practical Guide to Governing at the Grassroots*, Armonk, NY: M.E. Sharpe Pubishers.

Clarke, S. E., & Kirby, A. (1990, March). In Search of the Corpse: The Mysterious Case of Local Politics. *Urban Affairs Quarterly, 25*(3), 389–412.

Clavel, P. (1986). *The Progressive City*. New Brunswick, NJ: Rutgers University Press.

Clawson, D., & Al., E. (Eds.). (2007). *Public Sociology: Fifteen Eminent Sociologists Debate Politics and the Profession in the Twenty-First Century*. Berkeley: University of California Press.

Colburn, J. E. (2006). Localism's Ecology: Protecting and Restoring Habitat in the Suburban Nation. *Ecology Law Quarterly, 33*, 945–1014.

Community Sustainability Award. (2008, October). *Public Management, 90*(9), icma 16 icma27.

Cox, K. R. (1999). Ideology and the Growth Coalition. In A. E. Jonas & D. Wilson (Eds.), *The Urban Growth Machine: Critical Perspectives, Two Decades Later* (pp. 21–36). Albany: State University of New York Press.

Cox, K. R., & Mair, A. (1988). Locality and Community in the Politics of Local Economic Development. *Annals of the Association of American Geographers, 78*(2), 307–325.

Dahl, R. (1961). *Who Governs? Democracy and Power in an American City*. New Haven: Yale University Press.

Darnovsky, M., Epstein, B., & Flacks, R. (1995). *Cultural Politics and Social Movements*. Philadelphia: Temple University Press.

Domhoff, G. W. (2010). *Who Rules America?: Challenges to Corporate and Class Dominance* (Sixth Edition ed.). New York: McGraw Hill.

Donovan, T., & Neiman, M. (1992, September). Citizen Mobilization and the Adoption of Local Growth Control. *Western Political Quarterly, 45*(3), 651–675. Retrieved from http://wwwjstor.org/stable/448686

Duany, A., Plater-Zyberk, E., & Speck, J. (2000). *Suburban Nation: The Rise of Sprawl and the Decline of the American Dream*. New York: North Point Press.

Duffy, K. J. (2014, Summer). Regulating Hydraulic Fracturing Through Land Use State Preemption Prevails. *University of Colorado Law Review, 85*(3), 817–865.

Duncan, J., & Duncan N. (2003). Can't Live With Them; Can't Landscape Without Them: Racism and the Pastoral Aesthetic in Suburban New York. *Landscape Journal, 22*(1), 88–98.

Duncan, J., & Duncan, N. G. (2004). *Landscapes of Privilege: The Politics of the Aesthetic in an American Suburb*. New York: Routledge.

Dye, R. F., & Reschovsky, A. (2008, Summer). Property Tax Responses to State Aid Cuts in Recent Fiscal Crisis. *Public Budgeting & Finance, 28*(2), 87–111.

Dye, T. R. (1994). *Politics in States and Communities* (Eighth ed.). Englewood Cliffs, NJ: Prentice-Hall (Original work published 1969).

Edwards, A. R. (2015). *The Sustainability Revolution*. Gabriola Island, BC: New Society Publishers.

Feagin, J. R., & Sikes, M. P. (2008). Navigating Public Places. In *Intersections: Readings in Sociology* (pp. 189–203). Boston, MA: Pearson. (Reprinted from *Intersections: Readings in Sociology*, by B. Truchil)

Fernandez, R., & Rogerson, R. (1996, February). Income Distribution, Communities, and the Quality of Public Educaiton. *The Quarterly Journal of Economics, 111*(1), 135–164.

Fischel, W. A. (2004, February). An Economic History of Zoning and a Cure for its Exclusionary Effects. *Urban Studies, 41*(2), 317–340. doi:10.1080/0042098032000165271

Flatt, V. B. (2008). Act Locally, Affect Globally: How Changing Social Norms to Influence the Private Sector Shows a Path to Using Local Government to Control Environmental Harms. *Boston College Environmental Affairs Law Review, 35*(3), 455–478.

Flacks, R. (1995). Cultural Politics and Social Movements. In M. Darnovsky, B. Epstein, & R. Flacks (Eds.), *Think Globally, Act Politically: Some Notes toward New Movement Strategy* (pp. 251–263). Philadelphia: Temple University Press.

Finkelstein, E., & Zuckerman, L. (2008). *The Fattening of America*. Hoboken, NJ: John Wiley and Sons.

Fosler, R. S. (Ed.). (1999). "The Suburban County." In R. L. Kemp (Ed.), *Forms of Local Government* (pp. 117–121). Carolina: McFarland & Company, Publishers.

Fraser, J. C., & Kick, E. L. (2007, November). "The Role of Public, Private, Non-Profit Community Sectors in Shaping Mixed-Income Housing Outcomes in the US." *Urban Studies, 44*(12), 2357–2377.

Freeman, R. J., Shoulders, C. D., & Allison, G. S. (2006). *Governmental and Non-profit Accounting* (Eighth ed.). Upper Saddle River, NJ: Pearson Prentice Hall. (Original work published 1993).

Gaffney, M. M. (1971). "The property Tax is a Progressive Tax." In *Sixty-Fourth Annual Conference on Taxation sponsored by the National Tax Association. Proceedings of the Sixty-Fourth Annual Conference on Taxation* (pp. 408–426). National Tax Association.

Gallagher, L. (2013). *The End of Suburbs*. New York: Portfolio/Penguin.

Gans, H. J. (1967). *The Levittowners: How People Live and Politic in Suburbia*. New York: Panthoein Press.

Gans, H. J. (1982). *The Urban Villagers*. New York: The Free Press.

Gendron, R., & Domhoff, G. W. (2009). *The Leftmost City: Power and Progressive Politics in Santa Cruz*. Boulder, CO: Westview Press.

Gianakis, G. A., & McCue, C. P. (1999). *Local Government Budgeting*. Westport, CT: Quorum Books.

Gottdiener, M. (1994). *The New Urban Sociology*. New York: McGraw-Hill.

Greene, J. D. (1999, Winter). Privatization Popular Among Local Governments. *Montana Business Quarterly*, 17–20.

Griffin, B. W. (1981). *Cities Within a City: On Changing Clevelnd's Government.* Cleveland: Cleveland State University, Special Reports in Urban Affairs Series.

Grindle, M. S. (2007). *Going Local: Decentralization, Democratization, and the Promise of Good Governance*. Princeton, NJ: Princeton University Press.

Hanrahan, J. D. (1977). *Government for Sale: Contracting Out the New Patronage*. Washington, DC: American Federation of State, County and Municipal Employees.

Harless, J. (2002, January/February). Local Government Environmental Advisory Boards. *Journal of Environmental Health, 64*(6), 30–32.

Hawkins, C. (2011, March). Electoral Support for Community Growth Management Policy. *Social Science Quarterly, 2*(1), 268–284.

Hawkins, C. (2014). Competing Interests and the Political Market for Smart Growth Policy. *Urban Studies, 51*(12), 2503–2522. doi:10.1177/0042098013512875

Heiman, R. (2015). *Driving After Class: Anxious Times in an American Suburb.* Oakland, CA: University of California Press.

Hess, D. J. (2009). *Localist Movements in a Global Economy: Sustainability, Justice, and Urban Debelopment in the United States*. Cambridge, MA: The MIT Press.

Hirt, S. A. (2014). *Zoned in the USA*. Ithaca: Cornell University Press.

Humphrey, C. R. (2001, March). Disarming the War of the Growth Machine. *Sociological Forum, 16*(1), 99–121.

Incarvaia, J. (2003, January). Reserves are Essential to Fiscal Health. *American City & County, 118*(1), 8.

Jackson, K. (1987). *Crabgrass Frontiers*. New York: Oxford University Press.

Jonas, A. E., & Wilson, D. (Eds.). (1999). *The Urban Growth Machine: Critical Perspectives, Two Decades Later*. Albany: State University of New York Press.

Kanter, R. M. (2015). *Move: Putting America's Infrastructure Back in the Lead.* New York: W.W. Norton and Company.

Kemp, R. L. (Ed.). (1999). *Forms of Local Government.* Jefferson, NC: McFarland & Company, Publishera.

Klein, N. (2014). *This Changes Everything: Capitalism vs. The Climate*. New York: Simon and Schuster.

Kolko, G. (1965). *Railroads and Regulation: 1877–1916.* New York: W.W. Norton.

Knox, P. L., & Mayer, H. (2009). *Small Town Sustainability: Economic, Social and Environmental Innovation*. Basel, Switzerland: Birkhauser Verlag AG.

Knox, P. L. (2008). *Metroburbia USA*. New Brunswick, NJ: Rutgers University Press.

Kozol, J. (1991). *Savage Inequalities*. New York: Crown Publishers.

Krugman, P., & Wells, P. (2015). *Microeconomics* (Fourth ed.). New York: Worth Publishers.

Lameiros, M. (2007, January). Take Action to Limit Eminent Domain. *American City & Government, 122*(1), 8–10.

Lancaster, L. W. (1931, December). Our Scrambled Local Government. *The North American Review, 232*(6), 559–568.

Land, K. (2008). "Whither Public Sociology?" *Contemporary Sociology, 37*(6), 507–511.

Lang, R. E., & Sohmer, R. R. (2000). Editor's Introduction. *Housing Policy Debate, 11*(2), 291–298.

Levitt, B. B., & Lai, H. (2010). Biological Effects from Exposure to Electromagnetic Radiation Emitted by Cell Tower Base Stations and Other Antenna Arrays. *Environmental Reviews*, 2010, *18*(NA): 369–395. https://doi.org/10.1139/A10–018

Lobao, L., Adua, L., & Hooks, G. (2014). Privatization, Business Attraction, and Social Services across the United States: Local Governments' Use of Market-Oriented, Neo-Liberal Policies in the Post-2000 Period. *Social Problems, 61*(4), 644–672.

Logan, J. R., & Molotch, H. L. (1987). *Urban Fortunes*. Berkeley: University of California Press.

Logan, M. F. (1995). *Fighting Sprawl and City Hall: Resistance to Urban Growth in the Southwest*. Tuscon: University of Arizona Press.

Lorch, R. S. (2000). *State and Local Politics*. Englewood Cliffs, NJ: Prentice-Hall.

Loury, G. C. (2015, January 1). Ferguson Won't Change Anything. What Will? *Boston Review*. Retrieved from http://eds.a.ebscohost.com/eds/pdfviewer database. (sid=05a7e629–4268–406e-b031-f3a83f1b7fc0%40sessionmgr4003&vid=13&hid=4202)

Lubell, M., Feiock, R., & Ramirez, E. (2005). Political Institutions and Conservation by Local Governments, *Urban Affairs Quarterly, 40*(6), 706–729.

Lubell, M., Feiock, R., & Ramirez de la Cruz, E. (2009). Local Institutions and the Politics of Urban Growth. *American Journal of Political Science, 53*(3), 649–665.

Lynd, R. S., & Lynn, H. M. (1956). *Middletown: A Study in Modern American Culture*. New York: Harvest Books.

Manis, J. G., & Stine, L. C. (1958–1959, Winter). Suburban Residence and Political Behavior. *The Public Opinion Quarterly, 22*(4), 483–489.

Martindale, D., & Hanson, R. C. (1969). *Small Town and the Naiton*. Westport, CT: Greenwood Publishing.

Martinson, T. (2000). *American Dreamscape: The Pursuit of Happiness in Postwar Suburbia*. New York: Carroll & Graf Publishers, Inc.

Mattson, G. A. (2002). *Small Towns, Sprawl and the Politics of Policy Choices*. Lanham, MD: University Press of America.

Marx, K., & Engels, F. (1972). *The Communist Manifesto*. In R. C. Tucker, *The Marx-Engels Reader* (pp. 331–362). New York: W.W. Norton & Company.

McKee, S. and Teigen, J. M. (2009). "Probing the Reds and Blues: Sectionalism and Voter Location in the 2000 and 2004 Presidential Elections." *Political Geography, 28*(8), 484–495.

Mendilow, J. (2012). Introduction: Political Finance, Corruption, and the Future of Democracy. In J. Mendilow, *Money, Corruption, and Political Competition in Established and Emerging Democracies* (pp. 1–16). Lanham, MD: Lexington Books.

Mendilow, J. (2012). *Money, Corruption, and Political Competiton in Established and Emerging Democracies*. Lanthan, MD: Lexington Books.

Mendilow, J., & Peleg, I. (2014). *Corruption in the Contemporary World*. Lanham, MD: Lexington Books.

Mendilow, J., & Peleg, I. (2014). Introduction: Edmund Burke's Concept of Corruption and Beyond. In J. Mendilow & I. Peleg, *Corruption in the Contemporary World* (pp. 1–26) [Introduction]. Lanham, MD: Lexington Books.

Mihaylov, N. L., & Perkins, D. D. (2015, March 23). "Local Environmental Grassroots: Contributions from Environmental Psychology, Sociology and Politics." *Behavioral Sciences, 5*, 121–153. doi:10.3390/bs5010121

Modarres, A., & Kirby, A. (2010). The Suburban Question: Notes for a Research Program. *Cities*. Elvesier Ltd. doi:10.1016/j.cities.2009.11.009

Molotch, H. (1976, September). The City as a Growth Machine: Toward a Political Economy of Place. *The American Journal of Sociology, 82*(2), 309–332.

Molotch, H. (1986, September). The City as a Growth Machine: Toward a Political Economy of Place. *American Journal of Sociology, 82*(2), 309–332.

Molotch, H., & Vicari, S. (1988, December). Three Ways to Build the Development Process in the United States, Japan, and Italy. *Urban Affairs Review, 24*(2), 188–214.

Murphy, T. P., & Rehfuss, J. (1976). *Urban Politics in the Suburban Era*. Homewood, IL: The Dorsey Press.

Musgrave, R. A. (1994, May). Is a Property Tax on Housing Progressive? *The American Economic Review, 64*(2), 222–229.

Nice, D. C. (1986). "The Policy Consequences of Political Corruption". *Political Behavior, 8*(3), 287–295.

"Nonprofit perceptions of local government performance in affordable housing". (2009). *International Journal of Housing Markets and Analysis, 2*(3), 253–262. doi:10.1108/17538270910977545

Oliver, J. E., & Ha, S. E. (2007, August). Vote Choice in Suburban Elections. *American Political Science Review, 101*(3), 393–408.

O'Toole, D., Marshall, J., & Grewe, T. (1996, December). Current Local Government Budgeting Practices. *Government Finance Review, 12*(December), 25–29.

Palen, J. J. (1995). *The Suburbs*. New York: Mc-Graw-Hill.

Peck, J. (2011). Neoliberal Suburbanism: Frontier Space, *Urban Geography, 32*(6), 884–919 doi:10.2746/0272–3638.32.6.884

Phelps, N. A. & Wood, A. (2011). The New Post-suburban Politics? *Urban Studies*, 48, 2591.

Philp, M. (1997). Defining Political Corruption. *Political Studies, XLV*, 436–462.

Pope Francis. (2015). *Encyclical on Climate Change & Inequality: On Care for Our Common Home*. Brooklyn, NY: Melville House Publishing.

Portney, K. (2005, September/October). Civic Engagement and Sustainable Cities in the United States. *American Society for Public Administration, 65*(5), 579–591.

Putnam, R. (2000). *Bowling Alone: The Collapse and Revival of American Community*. New York: Simon and Schuster.

Rehfuss, J. (1977, January/February). Suburban Development and Governance. *Public Adminstration Review, 37*(1), 111–120.

Riker, W. H. (1959). *The Study of Local Politics*. New York: Random House.

Ross, S., & Evans, D. (2003). The Environmental Effect of Reusing and Recycling a Plastic-Based Packaging System. *Journal of Cleaner Production, 11*, 561–571. doi:10.1016/S0959–652(02)00089–6

Rudel, T. K. (2009). How do People Transform Landscapes? A Sociological Perspective on Suburban Sprawl and Tropical Deforestation. *American Journal of Sociology, 115*(1), 129–154.

Saha, D. (2009, January). Empirical Research on Local Government Sustainability Efforts in the USA: Gaps in the Current Literature. *Local Environment, 14*(1), 17–30.

Schneider, M. (1992, February). Undermining the Growth Machine: The Missing Link between Local Economic Development and Fiscal Payoffs. *The Journal of Politics, 54*(1), 214–230.

Schnore, L. F., & Alford, R. R. (1963, June). Forms of Government and Socioeconomic Characteristics of Suburbs. *Administraiton Science Quarterly, 8*(1), 1–17.

Seligman, E. R. A. (1890, March). The General Property Tax. *Political Science Quarterly, 5*(1), 24–64.

Short, J. R. (1999). Urban Imagineers: Boosterism and the Representation of Cities. In A. E. Jonas & B. Wilson (Eds.), *The Urban Growth Machine: Critical Perspectives, Two Decades Later* (pp. 37–54). Albany: State University of New York Press.

Sirianni, C. (2009). *Investing in Democracy: Engaging Citizens in Collaborative Governance*. Washington, DC: Brookings Institution Press.

Sole-Olle, A., & Viladecans-Marsal, E. (2013). Do Political Parties Matter for Local Land Use Policies? *CESfilo Working Paper*, No. 4284.

Smith, K. B. (1996). Sustainable Local Democracy. *Public Administration and Development, 16*, 163–178.

Smith, K. B., Greenblatt, A., & Buntin, J. (2005). *Goverining States & Localities*. Washington, DC: Congressional Quarterly Press.

Stanfield, R. L. (1979, Winter). Toward and Urban Policy with a Small-Town Accent. *Publius, 9*(1), 31–43.

Stansberry, M. (2005, March). It's Not Easy Being Green. *American City and County, 120*(3), 40–44.

Svensson, J. (2005, Summer). Eight Questions about Corruption. *The Journal of Economic Perspectives, 19*(3), 19–42.

Syed, A. (1966). *The Political Theory of American Local Government*. New York: Random House.

Tang, S. Y., Rubio-Cortes, G., Callahan, R., Pisano, M., & McGrath, M. (2014, Fall). Key Findings of Fiscal Sustainability for Local Governments in Southern California. *National Civic Review, 93* 3–14. doi:10.1002/ncr.21201

Tang, S. Y., Rubio-Cortes, G., Callahan, R., Pisano, M., & McGrath, M. (2014, Fall). Key Findings on fiscal Sustainability for Local Governments in Southern California. *National Civic Review*, 1–13. doi:10.1002/ncr.21201

Tarlock, A. D. (1993, Spring). Local Government Protection of Biodiversity: What Is Its Niche? *The University of Chicago Law Review, 60*(2), 555–613.

Teachout, Z. (2014). *Corruption in America: From Benjamin Franklin's Snuff Box to Citizens United*. Cambridge, MA: Harvard University Press.

Teaford, J. C. (1979). *City and Suburb: The Political Fragmentation of Metropolitan America, 1850–1970*. Baltimore: Johns Hopkins University Press.

Teaford, J. C. (2008). *The American Suburb: The Basics*. New York: Routledge.

The Yale Law Journal Company, Inc. (1970, April). The Constitutionality of Local Zoning. *The Yale Law Journal, 79*(5), 896–925.

Tonglet, M., Phillips, P. S., & Bates, M. P. (2004). Determining the Drivers for Householder Pro-environment Behaviour: Waste Minimisation Compared to Recycling. *Resources Conservation & Recycling, 42*, 27–48. doi:10.1016/j.resconrec.2004.02.001

Truchil, B. E. (1988). *Capital-Labor Relations in the U.S. Textile Industry*. New York: Praeger Pubishers.

Vasi, I. B. (2007, Spring). Thinking Globally, Planning Nationally and Acting Locally: Nested Organizational Fields and the Adoption of Environmental Practices. *Social Forces, 86*(1), 113–136.

Vicino, T. J. (2008). The Political History of a Postwar Suburban Society Revisited. *History Compass,* 6(1), 364–388.

Vidich, A. J., & Bensman, J. (1968). *Small Town in Mass Society*. Princeton, NJ: Princeton University Press.

Walsh, M. L. (1997). *Building Citizen Involvement: Strategies for Local Government*. Washington, DC: International City/County Management Association.

Weiland, P. S. (1998, Summer). Environmental Regulations and Local Government Institutional Capacity. *Public Administrative Quarterly, 22*(2), 176–202.

Werner, S. (1983, March/April). New Directions in the Study of Administrative Corruption. *Public Administration Review, 43*(2), 146–154.

White, M. J. (1978, Spring). Self-Interest in the Suburbs: The Trend Toward No-Growth Zoning. *Policy Analysis, 4*(2), 185–203.

Wolf, R., & Wolf, D. (2004). Increased Incidence of Cancer Near a Cell Phone Transmitter Station. *International Journal of Cancer, 1*(2), 1–11.

Wu, Y. (2009, Winter). How Municipal Property Tax Responded to State Aid Cuts: The Case of Massachussetts Municipalities in the Post-2001 Fiscal Crisis. *Public Budgeting & Finance, 11*(3), 74–89.

Yerena, A. (2005). "The Impact of Advocacy Organizations of Low-Income Housing Policy on U.S. Cities". *Urban Affairs Review, 51*(6), 1–28. doi:10.1177/1078087415571451

You, J.-S., & Khagram, S. (2005, February). "A Comparative Study of Inequaity and Corruption." *American Sociological Review,* pp. 136–157.

Index

About the Author

Barry E. Truchil has been a sociology professor at Rider University for over 30 years. His primary teaching areas are political sociology and social theory. His previous book, *Capital-Labor Relations in the U.S. Textile Industry* examined how mechanization in the labor process and the movement of textile mills outside the country after World War II affected the relationship between textile capital and labor.

He has also been active in his community. He was elected to Langhorne Borough Council in 1991 and served as a member of council until 2009, most of which was as council president. He remains a member of the Historical Architecture Review Board (HARB) in the Borough. He was also president of the Board of Directors for The Peace Center, a nonprofit organization that promotes peace and social justice issues in Bucks County, Pennsylvania, from 2011 to 2015.

www.ingramcontent.com/pod-product-compliance
Lightning Source LLC
LaVergne TN
LVHW090755270926
848950LV00042B/23
* 9 7 8 1 4 9 8 5 2 0 4 4 7 *